How To Write A Book ASAP

The Step-by-Step Guide to Writing Your First Book Fast!

Garrett Pierson

How To Write A Book ASAP

First published in 2011 by New Generation Consulting LLC.
Copyright © 2011 by Garrett Paul Pierson.

All rights reserved. No part of this book may be reproduced or transmitted in any form or by any means (electronic, mechanical, photocopying, recording, or otherwise) without written permission from the author.

Limit of Liability/Disclaimer of Warranty: While the publisher and author of this book have used their best efforts in preparing this book, they make no representations or warranties with respect to the accuracy or completeness of the contents of this work with specific disclaimer of all warranties, including, without limitation, warranties of success for a particular purpose. The advice and strategies contained herein may not be suitable for your situation. Neither the publisher nor the author shall be liable for any loss of profit or any other commercial damages. The publisher and author are not engaged in rendering legal, accounting, medical, or other professional services.

ISBN: 978-0-692-01599-5

Printed in the United States of America

10 9 8 7 6 5 4 3 2 1

Contents

Introduction 5
Chapter 1. Mindset – You Have What It Takes! 9
Chapter 2. When to Write What 25
Chapter 3. Organizing Your Time 35
Chapter 4. Questions? Here Are Some Answers... 47
Chapter 5. Where's Your Book? 61
Chapter 6. Forming the Core 71
Chapter 7. A Psychological Shift 85
Chapter 8. Write NOW! 93
Chapter 9. The Publishing Fairytale 103
Chapter 10. Books Done! What's Next? 115
Continuing Education 131
About the Author 132

Introduction

"Hey Garrett! Thanks so much for the presentation today; it really motivated me to write my book soon."

"How soon?" I ask.

"Well, I'm not sure, but I really want to write a book, I think it will really help me become an authority in my market."

"I totally agree! So when are you going to write this book?" I inquire, digging deeper.

"I hope to get started soon."

I can't tell you how many of these conversations I've had with people at events where I have spoken or after presentations I have given.

Here is another conversation I often have:

"Hey Garrett! Thanks so much for the presentation today; it really motivated me to write my book soon."

"How soon?" I ask.

"I am hoping to get started tonight when I get home."

"That's amazing! So when do you plan on finishing the book?" I say.

"I want to finish the book by the end of November, do you think I can?"

"I know you can!" I respond.

I can almost guarantee that those people who aren't quite sure when they'll start still haven't written a word. However, those who give specific, honest and committed answers will almost always finish the book that they want to write.

I know exactly who will succeed and who will not.

So what would this conversation sound like if you were the person talking with me?

If you're reading this book then we can assume that you want to write a book, whether it be a novel or non-fiction. In Chapter 1 of this book you will better understand the importance of how your answers to certain questions will affect your success.

I still remember my first book "What Success Takes." I had no idea what I was doing, no clue how to write and no concept as to the time and effort it would take to finish. All I knew is that I wanted to be an author and had something to share with others. Come to find out that was all I needed. I was committed and nothing could stop me.

There are many mind-boggling and complicated ways of writing a book at our disposal. This is not one of those. In fact, this book is perfect for someone who wants a simple, flexible and streamlined approach to start, write and complete a book fast.

This is not a get rich quick book, nor is it a book that guarantees your success. That is up to you. I can't write your book for you.

This book is for those of us who want to write regardless of what others say about our ability to write. It is for those of us who want a step-by-step guide to the process and strategies to finishing a book. The book is specially formulated to be a tool to support your success. If you want to avoid mistakes and prevent costly pitfalls, whether those pitfalls be measured in time and/or money wasted, then this book is for you. This book is all about achieving real and practical writing results.

You will only become a writer/author through the act of writing. This is your golden opportunity to stop talking about writing a book and actually do it. Only when your book is finished will you truly understand the authority and respect authorship demands and how the title of "author' can open up new channels of achievement and profit.

You might find this book to be somewhat unconventional. There may be established writers who disagree with my writing style. That is to be expected since I do not come from the traditional writing world. You will soon learn my story and though I was an overall good student, I was a terrible English student. I know this might sound cliché, but if I can become an established writer, anyone can!

More than most people, I understand your concerns, anxieties and questions when it comes to writing. I've been where you are and know how to overcome the roadblocks you undoubtedly will encounter. That's why I wrote this book. To help guide you towards the finish line so that you can proudly hold your own book in your hands.

Here is what you can expect to learn while reading this book:

- All the right ingredients to get started
- Why you shouldn't start writing until you're ready
- Detailed strategies to organization and self-control
- A crash course in the basic writing process
- Rewarding yourself by shifting your mindset
- Clear steps to finishing your book fast and staying laser focused
- Traditional publishing vs. self-publishing and what is right for you

- How to become the authority in your market when your book is finished

- Plus much more

Don't delay! You've waited long enough. Let's get started, you'll be glad you did!

If you have any questions throughout the book make sure you ask them here – HowToWriteABookASAP.com/Questions

Also find out how you can join other authors like yourself in the How To Write A Book ASAP "Writers Circle" – HowToWriteABookASAP.com/Training

Chapter 1

Mindset - You Have What It Takes!

The Word document cursor was flashing and seemed as though it would never stop. I knew that writing my first book would be difficult. But, I was ready to face the challenge. As I sat there looking at the blank canvas, I got a little nervous. "Can I do this?" I thought to myself.

My mind went back to high school and college thinking of what my English teachers would say if I told them I was writing a book. I know what they would say. Better yet, I know what they would do - LAUGH.

You see, I was a great student. In most of my classes I got good grades and was involved in school activities. But when it came to English, I got C's and D's. I can't really put my finger on why, other than I just couldn't quite seem to get the concept of grammar. Oh, and I wasn't particularly fond of reading either.

The ironic thing is that although my teachers would probably laugh at the concept of me, Garrett Pierson, writing a book, I guarantee that most of them had never written a book and they taught writing! I wasn't going to let my English grades stop my desire to write.

After thinking about how my teachers might react, my thoughts went to my friends, family, and others who would read my book. "What if they didn't like it?" I thought to myself. "What if someone notices a spelling or grammatical error? If someone calls me out on something in my book, then what?" I was pretty much just being a baby. That's what it really came down to. Sometimes we think that if we could make everyone happy then the world would be a much better place. But the truth is that if we try to please everyone, our chances for success are pretty slim. I couldn't let what others thought or think stop me and neither can you.

The next roadblock I had to overcome when writing my first book was the inner monologue going on in my head. Doubt, anxiety, and the sheer lack of knowledge were intimidating. I didn't know how to write a book, nor did I possess the skills to do so. But the underlying truth was that I wasn't going to let my limitations and fears stop me.

Here's why: I made a commitment to write a book and therefore I wasn't going to give up. I have a saying that I have kept with me ever since I was a teenager. "Never Give Up." The truth is, I was scared. But nothing was going to get in my way.

We have discussed some initial challenges to writing your first book, namely concerns about what others think about us and our own self-doubts.

Here is what I have learned when it comes to other people's opinions; they're just that, their opinions or perspectives. If someone doesn't like my book then that is his or her right to have that opinion. But it doesn't mean that my book doesn't have value and won't help someone. The way I look at it is like this: when someone talks bad about my book then I have succeeded in creating a topic that somebody feels is worth discussing.

Here is a quick example illustrating what I mean. Howard Stern has millions of listeners. Guess who makes up the majority of his following? It's the critics that hate him. They want to hear what he has to say next. They're anxiously waiting for the opportunity to debate their point of view against his. Sometimes, I think he says things just to get a response out of people. Those who aren't critics who listen to him enjoy the differences of opinion, no matter which side they agree with on a particular topic.

We're about to change any negative thoughts, roadblocks or challenges into opportunities for success. Sound good?

Are you still staring at the blinking cursor on your screen? Have you written 100 words yet? Are you stuck and can't seem to move forward? It's OK. I'm here to help you get through any obstruction that might be in your way. In my opinion, the key to writing a book is quickly finishing it. If you don't finish the book what's the point? Your voice can't be heard and you can't help or entertain others if you don't yield a complete work.

It's no secret now that I am not a great writer. My English grades in high school and college were horrific. That seemingly important detail didn't thwart my ambitions, rather it made the end result sweeter; like an underdog transforming into a champion. Don't allow past negative experiences imprison your future opportunities.

I'm aware that past run-ins with the writing process aren't the only webs of regression. Everyday you have social and family activities, as well as jobs, church assignments, community projects and school. And although these provide balance and are positive experiences for the most part, they can act as deterrents in completing your book. If you wish to accomplish anything in your life, including getting your book published, you must make time in your hectic schedule to do it. None of the events or excuses above has the power to stop you from writing because you have the authority to choose what to do with your time.

Allow me to illustrate my point with a parable. There were two wood vendors whose large carts sunk in the mud while trying to reach the market a few hills away. One was a cantankerous, closed-minded old man who sat upon his cart in defeat. The other man, just as old, surveyed the situation, organized himself, and used his wood to form a makeshift ramp then pushed the cart up and out of the mud. Although your proverbial cart might be stuck in sludge, I promise you that the market is only a few hills away. Keep an open mind and an optimistic attitude. Nothing can stop you. Forget what the world thinks – you can do this.

Let me tell you a story about Brad Burton, a man I dearly respect. His experience in writing his first book is another testimonial which illustrates that you can do this.

Brad is now a professional motivational speaker with charismatic magic and an exceptional, "welcome back, best friend" smile. Brad also has dyslexia, which is a learning disability that impairs spelling, sounding out, and recognizing words and letters.

When Brad set out to write his first book, you can imagine the fear and doubt that came to his mind. The task seemed insurmountable. If you were in Brad's shoes, would you even attempt to write a book if you had trouble handling even the basics of written English?

But with help from his coach and editor he overcame his fears and wrote an amazing book in the process.

His book, "Beyond Illusions" has become one of my favorites. He journeyed through the deep waters where every word was an enemy to the blissful shores of accomplishment by composing 127 pages of valuable, insightful content. He became an author!

If you want to hear more about Brad's journey in writing his first book go here – http://HowToWriteABookASAP.com/bradbarton.

I have heard of people who have been in the process of writing a book for years who still haven't finished and probably never will. I am not saying that you have to write your book in any certain amount of time. What I am saying is that if you set a goal and you commit yourself to it, more than likely you will triumph. For example, if you want to write your book in 90 days, set a goal to do so and go do it. If you want to write your book in one year then you need to have a good plan and break up the book into monthly chapters. Let's say you want to write your book in 3 days – the same process and mindset applies.

I could have started this book out by teaching you how to write and spell, but that would not have benefitted you one bit. How many of us know how to lose weight? I mean really. You take in fewer calories than your body can naturally burn and you exercise, it isn't rocket science, yet 90% of weight loss is mental not scientific. You won't lose weight if you don't choose to. You're in control!

My point is that you will never finish or even start your book if you don't have these key ingredients:

- A well devised plan/goal that you are conscious about daily
- 100% commitment to that plan/goal
- Consistent desire and follow through of your plan/goal
- MOST IMPORTANT – determined mindset

So what does it take to actually sit down and write your non-fiction book or novel? This is the kind of question that is destined to get a wide range of answers, as it can be seen from numerous different perspectives. However, at the end of the day, there is just no getting around a fundamental and simple fact. In order to finish any large task, whether it's simple or complex, you have to do it. This, of course, means that if you want to finish writing your book, you have to commit to dedicating the time necessary in order to make sure it happens.

It is an oversimplification to state that in order to finish your book you must write. There is more to it than that. You need to reorient your thinking. In short, you need to set aside the time to write. You absolutely must make writing, researching, organizing and other related issues in the writing of your book a priority in your life.

In chapter 2 we will begin to broaden your mind as to where you should start, for now, you have to start setting goals and come up with a specific plan on how you will obtain those goals.

Here are some simple yet powerful ways that you can set goals. They come from an article that my business partner Scott Brandley wrote for our Outstanding Ventures blog.

Step 1 – What do you really want?

When setting a goal, the very first question you need to ask yourself is "What do I really want?" and really think about it. Don't just make your goal, "I want to be successful" or "I want to get in shape" because it's too vague and there's nothing tangible to reach for or motivate you. You can do better than that. Try to make your goal more specific like, "I want to be earning $8,000 a month by January 1st, 2012" or "I want to run 5 miles without stopping by June 1st". This kind of goal will be a lot more motivational and give you something to work towards. It also gives you a target date.

Once you've decided what you really want, WRITE IT DOWN. It's one of the best ways to hold yourself accountable.

Whether you like it or not, writing down goals is critical to your success! In fact, in 1979 there was a study done with graduates from Harvard University. They were asked a simple question: "Have you set clear, written goals for your future and made plans to accomplish them?" The interviewers were surprised to find out that:

84% had no specific goals at all

13% had goals but they were not committed to paper

3% had clear, written goals and plans to accomplish them

In 1989, ten years later, the interviewers again interviewed the graduates of that class. The results were shocking:

The 13% of the class who had goals were earning, on average, twice as much as the 84 percent who had no goals at all.

Even more staggering – the three percent who had clear, written goals were earning, on average, **ten times as much as the other 97 percent put together**. (Source: from the book 'What They

Don't Teach You in the Harvard Business School', by Mark McCormack)

Write down your goals!

If you're saying to yourself that you don't have time to write down your goals, then how on earth are you going to have time to accomplish anything significant? Write your goals down!

Step 2 – Why do you want it?

Coming up with a compelling reason why you actually want to accomplish your goal is just as important as the goal itself. In most cases this is actually harder to come up with because you have to really think about the true motivation behind your goal.

Your reason 'why' is the catalyst that physically moves you towards achieving your goal. It is the power that pushes you to keep going when you don't think you can. It is what motivated the determined wood vendor to find a way to get to the market.

It's also a great way to see if you're setting the right goal. If you can't come up with a compelling reason to accomplish your goal, then you probably don't have the right goal.

Once you've come up with your reason or reasons why you absolutely must accomplish your goal, write it down directly underneath your goal.

Step 3 – How are you going to do it?

Remember the study that revealed that 3% of the Harvard graduates made 10 times more than all of the other 97% combined? Part of their incredible success was that they wrote down a plan to accomplish their goals.

This is the 3rd piece of the puzzle. You need to come up with a strategic plan on how you're going to accomplish your goal. It should include ambitious, but realistic milestones with attainable target dates next to them.

Now, this doesn't have to be a huge undertaking. It can be three milestones or ten. It can be three sentences or three pages – there's no right or wrong way to do it. The most important thing is to just write down what comes to you, because in almost every case, your first impressions will be right.

Step 4 – Exponentially increase your chance of success

Now that you've got your goal, your motivation, and your plan all written down, you're way ahead of the game, but you're still not out of the woods. There are <u>three more things you can do that will *exponentially increase* the likelihood of you successfully reaching your goal</u>.

Sign and date your goal – By signing and dating your goal you are creating a binding contract with yourself. The second you sign that paper, your mind will automatically start trying to figure out how to honor that agreement. After all, you just put your integrity and trust on the line, and nobody wants to breach a contract, right?

Tell someone about your goal – While it's very important to write down your goal, telling someone about it will help hold you accountable. It can often become easy to change or remove our goals when the going gets tough. But the odds of you following through increase significantly if you tell someone. And, just a quick side note, the more people you tell, the more likely you'll stick to it so it's best to tell several people.

Go for a daily 'Power Walk' – Power walks are special. They give you the ability to take a step back from your daily life and see the bigger picture. The best time to go for a power walk is right after you finish going to the gym or exercising. During my power walk I usually start out expressing my gratitude to my Creator for the blessings and opportunities in my life, including the opportunity to accomplish my goals. Then, once my head is

clear and I'm focused, I think of a goal and try to visualize accomplishing it, along with at least one way that I can make a small improvement in the next 24 hours in order to get one step closer to my goal.
And there you have it! This is the most effective way to reach any goal you can imagine.

What you should have realized by now is that your goals must be specific. Here is an example of what your goals could look like:

- I am writing a book about "Insert what your book is about" (Note this can change as you will find out in Chapter 2)
- I will write at least a 120 page book
- I will find an accountability partner or coach to help me by "specific date"
- I will write/finish writing my book by "specific date here" (ex. September 15th 20**)
- I will write 10 pages a day or I will write one chapter a week/month
- I will study/research for 30 minutes a day
- I will work on building up the main character of my story by "specific date"
- I will study my daily regimen and carve out the necessary time to write my book and will make my significant other and family aware of my goals by "specific date"

Obviously this is just a simple idea of what your goals and plan should look like. The more detailed you are, the more successful you will be, guaranteed. Make sure you read Chapter 3, where I share with you the exact goals and specific dates I created for writing this book.

Now you have a plan and have set specific goals. What's next?

To me this next item is the most important thing you will ever do in any aspect of your life. You and I must commit. My verb is "I Commit". What is your verb?

Every single time I have committed myself to something, I mean truly and honestly committed myself, I have succeeded 100% of the time. Every time that I haven't fully dedicated even if it was 98%, I have failed. Maybe you can relate.

Before you take any action you have to fully commit yourself to your plan and goals, 100%. If you waiver even a little on your commitment, you are setting yourself up for failure. Along with commitment comes conviction and dedication. Know that you can and will fulfill your goal. You must be a finisher, not only a starter.

At the heart of the issue of finishing your book is time management. Even if the issue that is causing you problems is the dreaded writer's block. You must dedicate time to writing in order to eventually work your way through the block. In many regards, writing is no different than many other endeavors in that it requires a significant amount of personal investment.

No one can expect to become a great piano player, painter, major league baseball player or a great "anything else" without a consistent investment of time. Even those who are gifted in a given area need to invest time in order to truly become great!

Thus time management is critical for your success as a writer, and time management is largely a product of your mindset. It's so important that I have carved out a whole chapter (Chapter 3) of this book, specifically focusing on this subject of organizing your time. So before you start writing make sure that you are aware of any environment and time constraints that you personally have. You may have to change your mindset regarding how you spend your time and your day.

At first, such a task may seem very foreign to you, especially if you do not like to structure your time. You might feel that such an activity is limiting and unnaturally 'robotic.'

However, reorganizing the time in your life is ironically liberating, not limiting, and is a key step in acquiring the mindset necessary to write your book!

The second key step is to believe that you can indeed finish! If you feel that finishing is impossible, no matter how hard you try, then you've instantly shifted your reality in that direction. After all, do you know anyone who has finished any major project when they believed all the while in his or her heart that it was impossible?

By reorganizing your time and believing that you can and will finish your book or novel, your chances for success will blossom. You will also discover that as you write more, your writing will become better, more polished and more of what you've always wanted it to be. Many people are intimidated by the act of writing, but if you want to be a writer, you have to overcome your fears!

Writers 'in embryo' say to themselves often, "I have written a book. I am an author. I have a voice in the world!" Vision, along with will-power, faith, determination and organization are all key aspects of "making it happen."

Remember that writing is usually a solitary act. While that means that you are the one in control, it also means that you have to motivate yourself. Part of this motivation is, of course, believing in yourself and realizing that with the right mindset, time and dedication you will in fact accomplish your goals! Your attitude truly is the deciding factor of your success. With this in mind, also know that you don't have to do it alone. In fact, you shouldn't do it alone. People that succeed have what others and I call an accountability partner. You may think of this accountability partner as a coach, mentor or teacher. The best person for this job is somebody that has finished what you are trying to accomplish.

Let's go back to the example I gave earlier of someone trying to lose weight. Having someone there who has lost weight cheering you on is going to significantly increase your chances of succeeding. My advice is to find someone who has written a book and then ask him or her to help you. Once you have found someone, make sure that they are committed and consistent in helping you to accomplish your goal. Picking the wrong person could backfire.

Breaking down your book into numerous smaller chunks, such as chapters and sections within chapters, you will start off in the right direction. If you see your book as being a task rather than an opportunity, then you won't have much fun doing it. Change your thoughts from "I have so many pages to write," to "I want to write more today, but I hit my goal and I need to do other things."

By breaking down your book idea into a series of small steps, you will find that not only is the job no longer daunting, but it may even seem quite manageable. Once again, your entire challenge is one of perspective and mindset. With the right mindset, you will be able to welcome the opportunity of writing your book and accomplish the results that might just surprise you and others as well! Now that is something to get excited about!

Take a deep breath and relax! This book contains all of the secret ingredients you will need to succeed. Slow down and focus on your mind and not the book at this point. In fact, you could be in for a surprise when you learn that you shouldn't actually start writing for a while yet. We have some work to do on your brain first.

Here is what I need you to do: Stop thinking about writing the book and start thinking about finishing the book. That may sound strange, but stay with me here.

You need to trick your brain. It should come as no surprise that most people are more comfortable with talking as opposed to writing. Your brain is wired to allow you to speak in an easy and free flowing way. After all, you have been speaking and expressing your thoughts verbally since you were just a baby.

However, when you try to put words on paper, sometimes the brain stutters. As a result, the writing process tends to be nowhere near as fluid as the speaking process.

In order to write without any type of blockage, it is important to switch over your brain's "wiring." Try to focus on allowing ideas to flow from your mouth directly to your hand or cursor. Through this process, you will become more and more adept at allowing your hand/fingers to translate your mind's ideas. It might take practice, but you will find that the more you practice writing, the better you will be at it. Have you ever thought about speaking your book instead of writing it? Think about that. I'll discuss this option further in another chapter.

You are likely familiar with the data processing associated with the right and left hemispheres of your brain. In general, the right side of your brain tends to be more emotional, intuitive and creative. On the other hand, the left side of your brain deals with logic and order. One issue that keeps many people from writing in a productive manner is that the right and left sides of their brain conflict with each other.

Creating a sense of flow when you are writing is no problem for the right side of your brain. In fact, if it were up to the right side of your brain, you would likely never encounter writer's block.

However, the left side of your brain is in charge of critical thinking. As such, its job is to edit, scrutinize and criticize your work. Have you ever sat down, attempting to write, but quickly found yourself throwing in the towel? Perhaps you began telling yourself, "This isn't good enough! I should give up." If so, these thoughts were stemming from the left side of your brain.
Further, the left side of your brain will also start to scrutinize your spelling and grammar. These issues can also shut down the free flow of ideas that are necessary for writing. Later on, we'll discuss some strategies to help you write faster.

One of the keys to writing your book is to realize that the different hemispheres of your brain are working against one another. Instead of letting your brain "battle it out," the trick is to start taking advantage of your brain's potential. Let the right side of your brain win and you will find success in writing a book.

When you allow yourself to break free from your internal critic, you will find that the end result is not only more creativity, but also of a higher level of quality.

Let's return to my statement, "Stop thinking about writing the book and start thinking about finishing the book" and talk about it for a moment.

Stop – This powerful word means to "abandon a specified practice or habit." - http://oxforddictionaries.com/definition/stop

Thinking about writing the book – right now we are not going to focus on starting the writing process. This will come later.

Start – Dictionary definition: "embark on a continuing action or a new venture." - http://oxforddictionaries.com/definition/start

Thinking about finishing the book – if you create a strong enough image in your mind of the finished product, you will finish it. Essentially your brain will do everything in its power to create what is necessary to finish your book. So bottom line, for the moment, focus on finishing and not on starting.

You might be concerned about other important details such as marketing your book, publishing your book and selling your book. Remove them from your mind at this point. Why worry about marketing and selling a book that doesn't exist yet? Worrying can move you away from creating a plan and committing yourself to writing the book.

Of course marketing and publishing your book are important, but not until you have the book in your hand. Don't let worrying about anything delay you in reaching your goal. Move forward. Keep telling yourself: "I will share my complete and finished message (or story) with the world!" If you think it will help, print that statement or one similar to it in big bold letters to remind you of your commitment to finish your book.

Chapter 2

When to Write What

Every great journey needs two things. The first is a destination. Without a destination (or to be less metaphorical, a goal) one is hopelessly lost. After reading Chapter 1, you are well aware of the importance of goals. Picking the right destination means selecting the topic or book idea that works best for you at this time in your life.

The second thing you need for a successful writing journey is to choose the right strategy. One needs to think about what type of project is the right fit, whether it be a novel or a non-fiction book. While it would be nice to think that you can write about anything under the sun, reality dictates otherwise. If you aren't a chemist, for example, you probably won't be tackling a book on chemistry. On the other hand, if you are truly interested in an area in which you have had no previous experience, researching and writing about what you have uncovered is one way to become respected in that field.

What?

It is a simple yet looming question. **What** is it that you will write about?

Before sitting down and writing, it is necessary that you choose a topic that fits with your knowledge base, skill set and, most importantly, your passion. Working inside the parameters of your knowledge base or skill set could seem limiting. But it is important to understand whether or not you have the knowledge necessary to write on a given subject. This begs the question "Is there a way around all of this?"

There are ways around working within the confines of your current knowledge. One way is to learn more about the given subject you wish to write about. Depending on the complexity of the subject, this may involve a short to moderate amount of time invested in learning more about the topic at hand.

However, if the subject matter is complex, further education, training and research are needed. If you want to venture outside of your natural comfort zone you should be prepared to sacrifice additional time and effort for additional preparation, whether it's informal or formal in nature.

Selecting a topic with which you are comfortable and familiar will drastically cut down on the time it takes to write your fiction, non-fiction, short story, book of poetry, prose or any other written work. Understanding what it is that you are capable of writing about is a vital part of the process.

Writers are human, after all, and that means they are subject to becoming frustrated just like everyone else. If you select a writing topic that you are not comfortable with or that is outside your comfort zone, you will face additional challenges and may face writer's block more often than if you had chosen a more well-known topic.

Let's say your desire is to write a short story or novel. Do you have any idea how to create a character, plot or storyline? You may want to learn more about these important aspects of a novel before you begin writing. Reading novels is much different than writing them. That being said, a person who enjoys reading novels should know how to write them better than the person who does not.

I have teamed up with Jeff Gerke who has been in the publishing business since 1994, is the author of six published novels, the staff editor for three publishing houses, a writer's conference teacher and most importantly, he has written books on how to write novels. If you need help writing a novel or short story, visit HowToWriteABookASAP.com/jeff to find out more about his program and how he can help you.

If you want to write non-fiction or a "how-to" book, I suggest you learn more about my full platinum training program at HowToWriteABookASAP.com/training.

Whether you're writing non-fiction or a novel, the process and mindset are almost identical. Neither style of book will be written unless you are committed and have a detailed plan in place.

The "what" of your book is going to play an enormous part in the process of writing and finishing your book. When you choose the right "what," there is a psychological or subconscious acceptance within you that will set in motion a desire, energy, and high level of enthusiasm to accomplish the work. Choosing the right topic will provide you with the power and ability to stay focused and committed.

You absolutely must be inspired, at least on some level, about the topic you are writing to successfully engage your readers. If you lack a basic enthusiasm for a topic, it will be very difficult to get your readers excited about that topic as well. Just like we can envision when someone is smiling when talking to them over the phone, our goal is to have our readers envision what we are thinking and feeling.

You might already know what you are going to write about. All I'm asking is that you make sure that you are extremely confident in the "what" at this point of your journey.

Here are some ways that you can be 100% convinced that the subject of your book is aligned with your goals and desires.

- You feel a sense of urgency to write about the subject at hand
- You can visualize the book in your hands
- You can easily articulate to others what your book will be about
- The subject and/or characters come easy to you, even naturally

- Putting together a one paragraph (and no more) description of your book takes you less than two minutes
- You not only believe that you can write about this subject, you know you can
- You feel confident that people will learn or be entertained by its content
- You can create content that is unique on the subject, and/or you can tell unique stories that relate to the reader and the subject
- You feel there is a need for your take on the subject/story in your market/niche
- You feel obligated to write about this topic or theme
- You will write until you are finished

I could go on and on and on, but the statements above are powerful and essential to your journey and destination. Not all of them will apply, but most will dictate whether or not you are comfortable with the path you are creating.

Demand excellence from yourself and you will obtain brilliance.

Remember the story about my first book that I started telling you about in Chapter 1? Well, let's bring an end to the story. The title of my first book was "What Success Takes" and, yes, I finished the book. In fact, I had a goal to finish the book in thirty days and I did. In the chapters that follow I will explain exactly how I did it and give you the process of how I write and how my writing style can help you. I will never forget the feeling of accomplishment that I felt when I received the book hot off the press! It was a feeling that changed everything. Every book I have written since then continues to give me that same sense of achievement and joy.

Knowing what I now know, I probably would have never written on the subject of "success," but I am very glad that I did. The book changed my life forever and I am very proud of what I accomplished. Is the book perfect? No. Was it a New York Times Best Seller? No. Yet it has brought more business and more authority to my life than I would have ever imagined. You see, writing a book puts you on a whole new level that has the potential to skyrocket your success. When you say that you are an author, people look and treat you differently (even if you got C's and D's in English).

Writing my first book when I was 27 years old gave me a leg up in my market and niche. Sure, I could have written more of a narrow/niche related book. The subject of "success" was very broad. But since then I have written and continue to write on more niche-related subjects.

For example, my second book I co-authored was titled, "The Trust Factor - 7 Secrets To Converting Your Online Visitors Into Lifetime Customers." It is all about how to build trust online and increase sales. This fits perfectly with what it is I currently do for a living which is to create and sell software that helps businesses improve the capacity of their customers to trust them, thereby increasing their sales.

Another book I have written, the book you are reading now is titled, "How To Write A Book ASAP - The Step-by-Step Guide To Writing Your First Book Fast." How is that for being laser-targeted on a subject or niche?

One point that would be easy to miss in this discussion of "when to write what" is that of knowing whether or not a given subject or story line is the appropriate subject for you to write about at this particular time in your life. Once you begin exploring ideas for your book, you may discover that whatever is the "most logical" fit for you to write about just doesn't appeal to you at this moment in time. Or, maybe you just can't write about it now due to family or financial reasons or maybe your market isn't ready for a book like this yet.

Sometimes projects are better left on the sidelines until the time is right. It can take months or sometimes years to find the best timing. Yet, it is important to remember that optimal timing can make writing a particular book far easier than it otherwise could be. If you are in tune with the topic you have selected, you will not have that frustrating feeling of "swimming upstream." This means that you can avoid many of the pitfalls that can accompany writing in general. This is particularly true when it comes to working on a large project like a novel.

Once you have selected a writing topic that is a good fit for you, it is important that you make strides in organizing your thoughts. Many writers feel that they can work without an outline or any plan for where their work is headed. With time, however, those writers tend to discover that in order to produce a cohesive and logically constructed book, an outline or plan of some sort is vital.

In the end, it all comes down to having a clear direction that will help you in your journey to success. Success will come by finishing your book and sharing your message with others.

How much?

This is the next question that needs to be answered. How much should you write? How long will your book be? At this point you may not have any clue, especially if you are writing a novel. I do, however, suggest that you come up with a rough estimate as to how long your book will be in pages or words.

In my opinion, a non-fiction book needs to be 100+ pages and a novel needs to be 200+ pages. There is no standard out there, mostly just opinions. But to me, anything less than 100 pages is simply too short to get your overall point across.

So how long is your book going to be? Write it down along with your other goals. Know that this can change and probably will. When I set out to write a book, my goal usually is 120 pages. Why? Because anything more than that, in my mind, is too much. People are super busy and want to read fast. For a novel on the other hand, people expect more than 120 pages usually and a lot of times it will take more than that to create your storyline and characters. So keep all this in mind and remember that it is simply my perspective – you may have different thoughts, and that is fine.

The average size book is 5.5 x 8.5 inches. This means that on average the normal letter size Microsoft Word document page that you are probably using to write will create 1.5 pages in a 5.5 x 8.5 inch book. That means that if you write 80 pages in Microsoft Word, for example, in most cases that will create 120 pages. You can write 80 pages, right? I think you can.

Now is the time to get a rough estimate of your book length.

Whether you are writing fiction or non-fiction, organization and structure are pivotally important. This is not to say that you have to create a rigid outline "day one" and stick to it all the way through. Your outline or plan can and should be adaptable, as you may make discoveries along the way that force you to rethink your work. Yes, this may lead to rewrites. But take it in stride because rewrites are just part of the writing process.

When?

You must know if now is the right time. You must know if now is the right time. You must know if now is the right time. That wasn't a mistake or editing error. I stated it three times to make sure that you are listening.

You cannot commit to anything if there is doubt or apprehension of any sort. By discerning your deepest thoughts, you will be able to know if now is right for you. If it is, then nothing is going to stop you. There will be roadblocks, of course, but if you know your purpose and the course is set, those roadblocks will simply be bumps in the road and not pillars of brick.

It should be pretty obvious by now that I am more concerned with your mentality and approach to writing then the actual process of writing. Chapter 1 was all about the "Why" and this chapter has been all about the "What" and "When" and the next two chapters will be more about "Where". The "How" is well towards the back of the book, which may frustrate you, but you will thank me in the end. Understand, I am doing this on purpose. You just have to trust me. The #1 mistake that I see first-time writers make is that they are focused on the wrong things. They are absorbed in the "How" and not on the "Why," "What," "When" and "Where." Think of the "How" as the vehicle that will get you to your destination and the "Why," "What," "When" and "Where" as the road to your final objective.

Often, beginner writers are so focused on writing and selling the book that they forget to create a plan of action. This usually leads to inaction and eventual failure. Without action, there is no book. It's that simple.

I am not going to let you fail. I am going to do my best to uplift and shift your thought processes by helping you recognize the importance of laying the ground work that is fundamental to writing and finishing your book.

If you have reached this point and have not written down your goals then take a moment and do so now. Commit yourself to a specific plan with exact dates. Take some time to be certain that the subject you want to write about is right for you and that now is the precise time to write on that subject.

I have found that people who have not followed the simple, yet essential steps outlined in this book have difficulty writing. I am confident that you will succeed as a writer with all the privileges, pride, and prestige that comes with it if you will heed my advice. More than likely you know how a diamond is created. Think of this book and my insistence to follow its guidelines as the pressure you need to create something beautiful and valuable.

Think of me as your accountability partner. I'm ready and willing, are you?

I'll get off my soapbox now. If you are still reading, you must be as eager as I am to make this happen. I know that you can do this. I was a kid who was uncomfortable writing – if I can do it, then anyone can.

I hope you can trust me because with trust we can make incredible things happen!

Is writing a book hard and time-consuming? Yes, I would be lying if I said it wasn't. It is also easy and the time goes by quickly if you know what you are doing. Getting started is as important as finishing, but make sure that you are getting started in the appropriate way.

Let's visualize your journey and destination for a minute.

Where are you going?

Why are you going there?

What are you going to do to get there?

When are you going to start?

Can you answer these four questions? If so, then you're ready to get started on the "HOW." Your next question should be, "How am I going to get there?"

Have you heard the analogy of a fighter pilot that got off course less than one degree and ended up hundreds of miles from where he was headed? Or, have you read about a train that left for a certain destination only to end up in a different city altogether because the conductor missed a single turning point. I recommend that you start on course and stay on course.

In the end, it is important to remember that you are in charge. The topic you select to write about is for you to choose. By selecting a topic that suits you, the entire process will feel more manageable and you will decrease your chances of writer's block and project-stopping malaise in writing. If you are excited, your readers will sense your excitement, often translating into an enormous amount of success.

Chapter 3

Organizing Your Time

Writing is magical when it is done well. But there is nothing inherently magical about the process of writing. If you believe that there is magic involved when you put pen to paper, you are in for a rough ride and may be shocked to learn that the magic only comes as a result of a lot of research, thought and revisions.

Successful writing is the result of good ideas, planning, rethinking of ideas and rewriting. Sitting down and expecting some sort of writing deity to inhabit your body and infuse you with the brilliance found only at the heart of the universe, will, except in very rare instances, fill you with disappointment. This is not to say that you can't become inspired and do exceptional writing when you are "in the zone." I believe that you can and that you will produce something of immense value. However, expecting words to just come to you is a lot like a baseball player who expects to show up on game day and hit home runs every time he's at bat without ever practicing. With dedication to the project, you can become an inspired writer.

At the heart of good writing, you will find what is at the heart of every creative endeavor: time management. Even painters who believe that they simply tap into the energy of the universe and create great paintings in a de facto blissful trance still have to set aside the time to produce their work. Thus, the foundation of your writing success is time management. Now that might not sound sexy and appealing, but it is nonetheless true.

Providing yourself with the time required to write is critical to writing for numerous reasons. Clearly, producing a finished work can only be attained by consistently spending the hours needed to write your book. Secondly, if you are not constantly writing, swinging the bat – so to speak – you can't improve your writing either. Reading can help, but writing helps more. It's the difference between watching someone hitting a base hit and hitting one yourself. Reading can help you learn writing styles that have made others successful. Writing will help you learn your own writing style. Commit yourself to make time for those things that are truly important to you. Simply saying that writing is important to you and that you want to be a writer is a far different animal than actually making the necessary sacrifices to write.

The first thing that you will need in order to organize your time to fit those precious writing hours into your schedule is a dedication to writing itself. You must be determined to find the time to write <u>no matter what</u>. Of course, there are bound to be some unforeseen exceptions. Don't fool yourself into believing that missing your goal of writing nightly, for example, because of a family emergency, will halt you from accomplishing your goal. Determine to make time the next night to keep your commitment intact. Making the time to write means that you set aside some time every day.

What you do with your time is completely up to you. You are the captain of your ship. You can choose to play video games, watch TV, exercise, eat, sleep, spend time with family and friends, attend church, work, serve the community, WRITE YOUR BOOK or just sit on your butt and do nothing. I am going to give you some simple strategies to help you make choices regarding your time that will benefit your life the most.

One of the biggest questions that I get from my students is, "How do I find time to write my book with all my commitments (job, family, religion, community, etc.)?"

It is a great question, and can be followed up with more questions:

What do you want to do with your time? This goes back to what it is you want and why you want it. Do you want to write a book? Yes! Are you willing to carve out the necessary amount of time and energy to write and finish your book? Yes! Then the answer to the question "How do I make time?" is answered, simply, "Love and respect yourself enough to give yourself time enough to do what your really want to do."

We all have a lot to do, and we all have only 24 hours in a day. Some days are busier than others, but that is by our own choosing. So the key to organizing your time is to remember that the way you spend your time is your choice. If you have to go to school, it is because you are choosing to go to school. If you have to help a friend move from one house to another, it is because you are choosing to do so. Both of these activities are beneficial, but it is up to you to choose when or if to do neither or both. Ultimately, you are the leader – the commander in chief – of your life.

To write your book you may have to give up some things. When I wrote my first book, I chose to wake up at 5:30 a.m. every morning to write. I had to give up a couple extra hours of sleep in the morning. But I also chose to go to bed earlier. It didn't take me too many mornings to learn that sleep is very important and without it your time and effort will be significantly less effective. So, keep in the back of your mind that you need to be well rested when you write your book.

While writing my second book, I carved out specific times in the evening to write.

As I write this book, I am sitting at our family cabin. I have no cell phone service and no Internet to distract me. I specifically planned out my trip to the cabin so that no one else would be here. I scheduled it with my wife and ensured that she felt comfortable with me being gone. I gave myself a sufficient amount of time to ponder, research and devise a plan that would best help you.

This is where your preparation and objectives from Chapter 1 will come in handy and where you might need to be more specific when determining when you are going to write.

This process begins by taking a long and honest look at how you are spending each day.

Here is the good news. The odds are that even though you feel constantly busy, you are probably not maximizing your time. Few of us are! By taking a frank and honest look at how we are spending our time and then adjusting our actions accordingly to get more out of our days, we can take a massive leap forward in productivity.

Finding wasted or ill-spent time in our days provides us with the means to write. Some of the most obvious "time wasters" are, television, movies and other forms of entertainment. You might be thinking something along the lines of "but I use entertainment to relax." While this might be true, the act of relaxing and the act of realizing our goals have two different outcomes. With the former we feel rested, with the later we feel invigorated and motivated to relax less!

A recent report by The Bureau of Labor Statistics states that in 2010, the average American spent 2.7 hours a day watching TV (http://www.bls.gov/news.release/atus.nr0.htm).

I think you can give up some TV to write your book

Evaluating how you spend your time is an exercise that you should consider by sitting down and writing it all out. This will help you focus your thinking and give you a visual and easily referenced way to consider how you are spending your time. Such an exercise may benefit you in ways that radiate beyond your writing as well. Once you see how you are spending your time, you can modify your schedule and find places in your day and week where you can set aside time to write.

Here is what I suggest that you do right now. Create a table and divide each day of the week into half hour increments. It should look something like this:

Organizing Your Time

	Sunday	Monday	Tuesday	Wednesday	Thursday	Friday	Saturday
12am							
12:30							
1:00							
1:30							
2:00							
2:30							
3:00							
3:30							
4:00							
4:30							
5:00							
5:30							
6:00							
6:30							
7:00							
7:30							
8:00							
8:30							
9:00							
9:30							
10:00							
10:30							
11:00							
11:30							
12pm							
12:30							
1:00							
1:30							
2:00							
2:30							
3:00							
3:30							
4:00							
4:30							
5:00							
5:30							
6:00							
6:30							
7:00							
7:30							
8:00							
8:30							
9:00							
9:30							
10:00							
10:30							
11:00							
11:30							

You can download a table like this at
HowToWriteABookASAP.com/schedule

Using your table, write down everything that you do on a daily basis every half hour of every week. Obviously some activities change week-to-week, but write down things that you do almost every week.

Now, look at the table and begin highlighting or crossing through non-essential activities. What is 'non-essential,' you ask? Anything that is not required for your innermost happiness. Essential activities are mostly associated with family, community and employment. I recommend that you cross through things that aren't making a significant impact in the betterment of your life.

Finding the time for writing may be easier or harder than you might think depending upon your particular situation. Spending the time with your children watching a movie, for example, can be a positive, bonding experience. But does it trump giving your children the example of someone who is sacrificing leisurely activity to achieve a personal goal? That's for you to decide. I recommend you take a good long and honest look at how you spend your time. Look for wasted time that could be spent writing. When you pause to assess your time, you may find that you honestly have very little time to spare or you may find that you have more time on your hands than you thought you did.

If you really want to write, you will find the time in your schedule to do so even if only for a few moments. Of course, with the stressors of day-to-day work, family obligations and other activities, finding the time to concentrate can be challenging. Many writers find that waking up to write early in the morning (before anyone else gets out of bed) can be a good strategy.

Organizing your time means that you make arrangements and preparations. You should know when you are going to write ahead of time.

With a proper schedule in place, you can now work on plans to finish your book. Establishing a date by which you want to finish your book is the key. You may not be able to reach that exact date, but organization and a daily rededication to finishing it will keep you on target. If you become significantly off target, get over it by setting a new, realistic yet challenging date and move on.

Writing involves planning. When you organize your time to write, you have given yourself the opportunity to arrange your thoughts. That is when the real writing begins!

Here are some of the steps that I take when organizing my time for writing:

1) Set specific date (ex. September, 21st)
2) Set specific time (ex. 5:30am to 7:30am)
3) Make sure that nothing will interfere with date and time (I review my scheduled activities the day before to see if anything will impede me from getting enough sleep)
4) Write the date and time on my white board
5) Enter date and time in my calendar on the computer and sync it to my phone
6) Write down the exact chapter(s) or topics that I will be writing
7) When required, create an outline to study and before the date and time scheduled to write. This usually takes another hour of my time. This will need to be scheduled with its own specific date and time
8) Begin writing at specific date and time scheduled
9) If something unforeseeable stops me from writing, set new specific date and time
10) Continue above process until my book is finished

This is what works for me. How you organize your time may be a bit different, but the end result should be similar. You may only want to write for 10 minutes a day, which is fine. You may want to write for 3 hours one day, take a day or week off and then do it again. It's up to you.

Back in Chapter 2, we talked about setting the length of your book. If you plan on writing a 120 page book (80 normal word document pages if your book size is 5.5 x 8.5), you are going to need to figure out how much time it is going to take you. Once you begin, you may find that it takes you on average 45 minutes to write one full word document page. This means that it is going to take you around 60 hours to finish your book. Maybe you're much faster and it only takes you 20 minutes to write a page, so you can plan on finishing your book in 26 hours. Keep in mind that these calculations are estimates based on a 120 page book.

These numbers may intimidate you or they may excite you.

Knowing these numbers may help guide you when organizing your time. They can also be helpful in determining a finishing date. If the project is going to take you 60 hours, and you work an hour every day, then you can estimate that your book will be finished in two months.

Here is a formula that I have created that may help you know how long it is going to take to write your book.

Formula: (# of pages you want your book to be ÷ 1.5) x average time to write one normal full MSWord document page in minutes ÷ 60 = hours of writing needed to finish book

Example: I want to write a 120 page book. I can write one normal full MSWord document page in about 35 minutes on average.

120 ÷ 1.5 = 80 pages
80 x 35 = 2800 minutes
2800 ÷ 60 = **47** hours of writing to finish your book

(Formula based on a 5.5 x 8.5 inch book with 11 font size, Times New Roman style,)

I have created a calculator that you can use to easily do the math above. Simply go to HowToWriteABookASAP.com/calculator

So let's say that it is going to take you 47 hours to write your book. If you write 30 minutes a day, then it will take you 70.5 days of writing to finish your book. If you write for 2 hours a day then that would mean you could finish your book in 23.5 days. Of course those days don't have to be consecutive. You could write every other day if you wanted.

What I am trying to do with all these crazy numbers is show you what you are up against so that you can have a solid plan to begin and finish each of your writing projects.

As I have mentioned before, getting started is half the battle. You need to have a very solid and specific goal on your start date to begin writing. Once you get the ball rolling it will be hard to stop it. Mainly because the more progress you make, the more desire you will have to finish it. You will get excited once you see the book taking form. For example, this is Chapter 3 of this book. The ball is now rolling for me and there is nothing that could stop me from finishing this book.

There is a psychological change that has given me energy and desire to keep writing and ultimately to finish. You'll learn more about this psychological shift in Chapter 7, and you'll know what I mean when you feel it too.

When are you going to start? It is an important question! Don't set the goal unless you know you will be ready to start. Remember, you must have committed yourself to finishing before you commit to starting. Most people do this the other way around. In these cases, the person commits to starting and maybe even does start, but they rarely finish. Once you have a specific date to start and finish, make sure you write them down.

Here is the "Seven Step Commitment Plan" you need to complete before you commit yourself to starting:

1) Commit to finishing the book by a specific date

2) Form a specific page/chapter/ topic plan and goals (written down)

3) Commit to a subject/storyline

4) Construct a title for your book (you can change it later)

5) Create chapter titles for book

6) Create simple outlines for each chapter

7) Stick to your word

Numbers 1, 2 and 3 above should have already been done by now according to previous chapters. Numbers 4, 5 and 6 are very new and might be somewhat confusing to you at this moment. You will learn more about these steps in Chapter 6, so don't worry.

If steps 1-7 above have been completed, then you can commit yourself to starting. I want to talk about starting now so that you will have a good handle on what to expect of yourself.

I'd like to be very transparent and share with you my goals and the plan that I have created for writing this book. This will hopefully illustrate some of the strategies that I have been teaching you.

Starting date October 1, 2011

>I commit to finishing my 120 page book on how to write books by November 5, 2011 (completed)

>I will create the title of my book on October 1, 2011 at 10am – 11am (completed)

>I will research what the market needs in regards to writing a book by October 8, 2011 (completed)

I will write my chapter titles on October 8, 2011 at 9am – 11am (completed)

I will create very simple 2 paragraph chapter outlines for every chapter by October 12, 2011 (completed)

I will find a copy editor to edit and proofread each chapter as I finish by October 12, 2011 (completed) – (more about editing will come in later chapters)

Next set of goals after the above have been completed:

I will start the writing process of my book on October 13, 2011 beginning with the first three chapters (completed)

I will begin cover design details and find designer by October 20, 2011 (you'll learn more about this in Chapter 7) (completed)

I will write 3 more chapters in the week of October 16, 2011 (before that week started I had planned out which days and times I would write) (completed)

I will write 3 more chapters in the week of October 23, 2011 (before that week started I had planned out which days and times I would write) (completed)

I will write chapter 10 and introduction on October 29 and 31, 2011 (completed)

I will read through the book and rewrite any areas that need improving by November 5, 2011 (completed)

This is exactly what I had written down before I even started anything, and I followed the plan exactly as written above. Was it a lofty goal to write my book in 36 days? Yes, it was! Did I know I could do it? Yes, I did! Were there obstacles that I had to overcome? You better believe it!

There is power in following the steps and strategies that I have been sharing with you. I truly hope that you recognize the big picture and the importance of the initial mindset and pre-writing strategies.

If I had just sat down at a computer and tried to start writing without the plan above, I can guarantee you that I would not have finished the book nor would I have given as much thought into its contents.

Let's recap the past three chapters to help you get organized:

- The mindset of when, what, why and where you write your book and not focusing immediately on the how, is essential to your success

- You need clear, specific, written goals and a carefully thought-out plan before you even start writing your book. Follow the "Seven Step Commitment Plan" before making a goal to start writing

- You must commit to finishing your book on a specific date before starting your book

- Clearly state what your book is about and know, without a doubt, before you start that the subject and the timing is perfect for you

- Evaluating how you spend your time each day will help you create the time needed to write and finish your book

Chapter 4

Questions? Here Are Some Answers!

There are many questions that new writers often ask when looking to tackle their first large project. Part of the process is asking the right questions. It is crucial to organize your thoughts so that you can prevail. The questions we are going to look at are nothing short of spectacular because they will help focus your mind on your project and clarify many key issues.

I have found the top five questions of "wanna-be" writers through extensive research and by talking to individuals who have the desire to write:

- How and where do I start?

- In what type of style should I write my book? Simple or technical?

- How long should my book be?

- First person vs. third person?

- Can I write a book without good writing skills?

While you may very well think of many other questions, these core five questions can serve as a marvelous launching point for thinking more about your writing, the writing process and what you ultimately wish to accomplish with virtually any writing project you undertake.

It is important to note that there are many different ways of approaching writing. Rules are indeed usually made to be broken – even shattered! Keep this in mind as you contemplate your own writing. Above all, remember that thinking about your writing and formulating a logical strategy and process is of paramount importance to creating a great final product!

How and where do I start?

"How and where do I start?" is a question that has caused countless writers a great deal of grief and sleepless nights! Often writers have trouble knowing where to start because they lack clarity of thought about the project at hand. With many first-time writers, there is minimal difficulty in knowing where to start and how to continue, once some clarity has been achieved. For this reason, the first three chapters of this book have focused on setting the groundwork to help you get started. If you are still worried about how and where to start then I highly recommend that you reread those first three chapters.

Having too many "unanswered questions," whether about characters, the relationship of characters to one another, character motivation or a series of other unanswered questions can serve as tremendous road blocks in the writing process.

When you have a firm idea of what you are actually writing about (the "what") and "where it's all headed," (the "why", "how much" and "when") then issues such as how and where to start usually take care of themselves in an organic fashion. It is this lack of clarity that can be the problem. This can be avoided by investing the time to chart out a clear outline and path for your writing project before diving in!

In what type of style should I write my book? Simple or technical?

Answering the question, 'What type of style should I use for my book and should it be simple or technical?' can be a complex and multifaceted question to answer. Here is why: Name any subject and there bound to be books about it. However, one writing style or formula does not work for all subjects.

Clearly, a book written on the history of mechanical engineering will differ from an actual book on mechanical engineering. Now just imagine how books differ when they are not on related topics! The style that you choose and your approach, no matter whether it is simple or technical, has to take into consideration the genre in which you are working. This fact holds true whether you are working on a first person novel or an academic work on mechanical engineering (or anything in between).

Picking the wrong approach and wrong style can derail your readers before they even have a chance to get to the meat of your story or your argument. Selecting the right tone and the right style is about more than choosing what you personally prefer. However, you must take your audience, your audience's expectations and the genre or topic being covered into consideration. Find books similar in content and context to what you're writing and review their style. Do some research, make a decision and stick with it.

How long should my book be?

Deciding how long your book should be depends on many factors. The forefront of your decision should be the issue of publication. Publishers generally don't want to see massive, lengthy books from first time authors (unless they are novels or technical in nature). When a publisher takes on a new author, it is a risky financial decision. After all, no matter how great they think your writing may be, they really only have their experience and instincts to help them make educated guesses as to how readers will react.

The bottom line is that your book's length should be determined by what you are looking to accomplish. If your ultimate goal is to be published by an established publisher, then longer books may not be in your best interest. In fact, publishers will likely request that you shorten your work if they are interested. If they are not interested, they simply won't read it in the first place! When it comes to publishers and publishing your book, don't fret. In Chapter 9 we are going to focus on this issue in much more depth. Remember, unless you are an established writer, finding a publisher only comes after there is a book (in most cases). I would have to say that the question of publishing is one of the most asked questions that I get.

When determining the length of your book you must realize that it is up to you. If you desire to write a 500-page book on "The Studies of Ancient Egypt", then do it. If you want to write a 75-page Book on "How to Train a Lizard," well, go for it. The key is to decide and then move forward.

"Garrett, I don't know how long my book should be and won't know until I write it." This may be true to some extent, but it has been my experience that a writer who has a grasp on his or her subject, develops an estimated number of pages for their book, and makes specific goals will almost always finish the book close to the number of pages projected.

What I am suggesting is that you just hypothesize on the length of your book and your mind will find a way to write it. Especially when that number is written down and you have committed to it. Can the number change? Of course!

Here is an idea: Research, research, research. Find out what your market/niche wants. Do surveys and polls, visit forums and message boards, and ask questions. Also look at other books in your market/niche and other related areas that may give you some ideas of how long your book should be. Warning! Don't get caught up in worrying too much and spending too much time researching. Why? Because your job is to write and finish the book, not try to do it like everyone else.

First person vs. third person?

First person versus third person is largely a matter of personal preference and how you want to impact your reader. First person perspectives in novels limit what the reader can possibly know. By contrast, a third person perspective is essentially "godlike," meaning that readers can know whatever the author chooses to provide them. The advantages of third person narratives are clear. However, first person allows for a more personal feel, touch and tone. This too is a question that you need to answer on your own. Without knowing what you are going to write about, I can't tell you which to use. It depends on your comfort zone. If you want to contact me after you have decided what to write about, my team and I would be more than happy to give you some suggestions. Simply visit HowToWriteABookASAP.com/questions.

Here are some questions to possibly help you decide.

Is your book a novel?
Is your book non-fiction?
Is your book an autobiography?

Ultimately it is your decision. I recommend you make it and move on.

If you are planning to write a novel or a short story, one of the first decisions you will need to make is what type of point of view you will use. Once you commit to using either first person, second person or third person, this choice will carry through your entire work. Therefore, making the right decision and sticking with it is crucial. You don't want to be regretting your decision halfway through writing your book! Many authors find that writing in the first person is not only easier, but is more beneficial overall.

In case you aren't familiar with what it means to write in first person, this is the type of book that is narrated by a character. In many books, a story is told in first person by a character that is not the main protagonist. This can definitely be an interesting literary choice. In a work written in first person, the reader is able to experience everything that the character experiences and knows. Through this process, you can convey many of the character's deepest and most personal thoughts and feelings. When you write in first person, you will end up using the words "I" and "me" a lot. A book that is in the genre of autobiographical fiction is also typically written in the first person.

Let's take a minute and compare what it means to write in third person. If you were to select this point of view, the story in your work would be told through an observer as opposed to someone who is experiencing the chain of events firsthand. As a result, objective and subjective reality are both described. In this case, you would end up using the words "he" and "she" when you refer to the characters.

There is also a second person point of view, but it is not used very often. The second person is when you describe characters as "you." One of the places you may have seen this exemplified is in the "Choose Your Own Adventure" books that you might have read as a child. Chances are that second person isn't ideal for your book or short story, as it could likely end up being very awkward to read.

There are a few drawbacks, however, to books written in the first person that you might want to consider before getting started. First of all, if there are subplots taking place that don't involve the main character, it may be difficult to figure out how to work them into the story. Another issue is that if you are writing a mystery or suspense book, it can be tricky to write in first person. Your main character, of course, will only know what he experiences, so it can be more difficult to establish tension by writing about things taking place outside his or her world. Again, with first person books, everything should be seen or experienced by the main character. With that being said, a third person narrator could be used to fill in any gaps.

One benefit of writing in the third person is that you can easily switch between what different characters think or feel. If you want to switch between different character's perspectives, however, it is imperative that you adeptly handle this to eliminate any potential confusion for the reader.

As it turns out, many books that are written in third person don't have very extensive character development. When it comes to fiction, readers tend to be drawn into a storyline when they really get involved with the characters. Books that only cover events and don't have strong characterizations often end up being boring to readers. One way to liven things up is by creating conversations between characters.

Some writers have found it beneficial to write one paragraph of their book in first person, then second, then third to see which they like better. Remember, the further along you are in the book the more difficult it is to make changes. Study it out in your mind before making any lasting decisions. Ultimately, the quality of your book will depend on your story, characters and overall writing ability, which leads us to our next question.

Can I write a book without superior writing skills?

As you gain experience as a writer, you will discover that your writing skills will improve. This is the case with almost any endeavor in life. Those who have felt remarkably un-athletic and never learned to play basketball, for example, have, with consistent practice and determination, gotten better with time. Writing is the same. You will improve with practice.

Remember my personal story in Chapter 1? I was a less-than-adequate writer when I wrote my first and second book. But my writing skills have vastly improved just by simply writing. I still have some grammatical errors, but I'm getting better every day. Keep in mind that when you do finish your book, it needs to be proofread and edited by someone else anyway. If grammar and spelling aren't your strong-suit, find someone with good writing skills (hopefully they got A's in English). The book you're reading now is not the same as it was when I first wrote it. It has gone through several renditions and corrections. In later chapters I will get into the important subject of rewriting and editing. First, your focus should be to take thoughts from your head and put them on paper as fast and as orderly as you can.

Here is something else to consider: most magazines and newspapers are written at a 3rd grade reading level. Can you believe that? When I first heard that I was ecstatic! You see, most people like to read fast and furiously, due to the culture of the fast paced world we live in. People read faster if their brains can comprehend the words more easily. Granted, you can't write a book on Molecular Science at a third grade level, but if you did, more people would probably read it. Think of the concept of the extremely popular "For Dummies" books. These are all written in a very basic format with lots of pictures for people to understand the basics of various subjects.

So, can you write a book without solid writing skills? Of course! Just don't expect your first draft to be your last draft. You should plan on making revisions and sifting through rewrites. In time, you will find that you can write a book even if initially you don't believe that you have the English skills to do so. Indeed, it is more important to believe first in yourself and stick to your commitments, knowing that you can and will get better, than it is to believe first in your writing, typing, or creativity skills.

We have just touched on the top five questions found to be most asked among people wanting to write a book for the first time. Here is one more that always comes up: Writer's Block.

If you have ever had writer's block, you already know what a frustrating situation it is. Sitting in front of a computer and looking at a blank screen can start to make almost anyone feel hopeless and depressed. If you are trying to write something by a designated deadline, writer's block can become even more grueling. As the hours go by and nothing appears on the page, would-be writers often feel like tearing their hair out! The good news is that writer's block can be cured. In fact, any writing project that you attempt can be completed by the deadline and goal that you have set.

First, let's take a look at what causes writer's block. It should come as no surprise that most people are more comfortable talking than they are writing. However, when we try to put words on paper, the brain often stutters. As a result, the writing process tends to be less fluid than speaking.

In order to write without any type of blockage, it is important to switch over our brain's "wiring." I recommend that you find a recording device and speak your ideas into that device. Go on a long walk and just pour your brain into that recording. This will utilize the natural way of speaking to get your ideas out of your head. Then you can get the recording transcribed or transcribe it yourself. I use Tamara Bentzur to do all my transcribing; you can find her at www.OutsourceTranscriptionServices.com. She is a bit more expensive than others, but she does an amazing job. You can also go to Elance.com. Just make sure that you find someone that speaks and writes your written language.

That's how I wrote my first book. I bought a nice microphone and started talking. Of course, I was talking in an organized way. I knew the chapter title and I had an outline. I simply talked about what I wanted to convey in that chapter. The recordings were transcribed and I went from there (I go over this in great detail in Chapter 8).

Speaking uses the right side of your brain, which is the creative side. Creating a sense of flow when you are writing is no problem for the right side of your brain. In fact, if it were up to the right side of your brain, you would likely never encounter writer's block, especially if you are a fast typist.

However, the left side of your brain is in charge of critical thinking. If we're not careful, it can scrutinize our spelling and grammar – shutting down the free flow of ideas that is necessary for writing.

One of the keys to overcoming writer's block is simply to realize that the different hemispheres of your brain are working against one another. Instead of letting your brain "battle it out," the trick is to start taking advantage of each side's potential. First, let the right side of your brain come up with creative content. Once this has occurred, you can allow the left side of your brain to edit and improve upon your work.

Here is an overview of what the process should look like:

1. Focus on opening the right side of your brain at the beginning of the writing process. Invite it to rule your mind.

2. Next create an outline for your chapter without letting the left hemisphere of the brain interfere. If you are writing a story, jot down some details about the characters and the plot. Try to get this step accomplished as quickly as possible.

3. Remind the left hemisphere of your brain not to worry about the details and that it can handle the technical side of your work later on.

4. If you find yourself beginning to worry about the quality of the content or the spelling and grammar, just take a deep breath and focus on letting these worries leave your mind. Just write. One tip that may work for you is to set a timer for let's say five minutes. During those five minutes you must write anything and everything creative that comes into your mind as if your life depended on it. As you progress as a writer, you will be able to move from five minutes to fifteen minutes and then to hours.

5. Finally, once your first draft has been completed by the right side of your brain, you can then feel free to access the left side of your brain to fine-tune your work.

When you allow yourself to break free from your internal critic, you will find that the end result is not only more creative, but also of a higher level of quality.

Another thing to consider is your environment. Where are you when you write? Are there kids running around, is the TV on? Do you have Facebook or Twitter up? Is your email or phone turned on? Are you looking out a window where there is a lot of activity unrelated to the book you're writing?

I remember when I was writing my first book. Gracie, now three years old, was just about to turn one. She was a sweet, well-behaved little girl but there was no way that I could concentrate on writing when she was awake. That is why I did my writing at 5:30 a.m.

The atmosphere you create will dictate the experience you have when writing. So, find a place and time where there are minimal distractions. Create a plan with specific dates and times that you will write. As I mentioned before, I am writing much of this book from our family cabin. There isn't a better place on earth for me. I have tried the library. That was a huge mistake; too many people and too many distractions. Another place that I recommend you avoid is Starbucks and cafés. Although it may work for you, the likelihood is that you could do more quality work elsewhere.

One more thing to ponder is the writer's diet. If you are hungry, it will be difficult to concentrate and write. Eat food that will give you a boost in energy, not weigh you down. Stay away from too much caffeine and sugar if you can, as this can cause too much energy in your body for you to be able to sit and focus your mind on the task at hand.

Consider also the amount of time you spend writing. If you have been writing for eight hours straight then you might very well hit writer's block because your brain has shut down. Be aware of this aspect of your writing process. You may need to write in shorter fragments of time. Take a break, eat an apple, go for a walk, and then get back to work. Sleep is also important, as I have mentioned before.

At times, we might need a little boost to get started writing. Sometimes this can come in the form of using other material for inspiration. Browse the Internet or look in a book and check out how other writers are handling similar projects. There is a lot of content out there and undoubtedly you should be able to find something that inspires you and leaves you feeling motivated.

One thing that writers often struggle with is figuring out a format for their work. If you can adopt some of the organizational strategies from other writers, you can create a template that can help guide your writing. Of course, make sure that any of your work that isn't original is acknowledged and cited. The point is to let others inspire and motivate you so that you, in turn, can more adeptly inspire and motivate others. Sometimes it is helpful to actually put another writer's text in your writing to guide you as you write. If you try doing this, be sure to delete anything that isn't yours during the workflow. This is just an idea to use if you get stuck. Once you get unstuck, stop researching and continue writing.

If you follow these guidelines, you will no longer waste hours of your life sitting in front of your computer without accomplishing tangible results. Remember; whenever you sit down to start writing, it is critical to use the left and right hemispheres of your brain to the best of their abilities. That means you need to first let the right side of your brain freely work on the content, and then allow the left side of your brain to make improvements. If you feel stuck, you can get a lot of mileage out of using other sources for inspiration.

Here is a list of some of the sources that I use for gathering inspiration when writing:

Magazines
Videos
Articles
News/Hot Topics
University Studies
Kids (you'd be surprised)
Asking people questions (surveys and polls)
Forums/Message boards
"Words That Sell" a book by Richard Bayan

There is an endless world of knowledge out there. More than likely the subject that you are writing about has already been researched and discussed by others. But this shouldn't stop you from writing your own 'opus' to help others learn, be entertained and even enlightened from your point of view.

Chapter 5

Where's Your Book?

Few feelings are more gut-wrenching than telling someone you're a writer and then not having a book to back it up. Anyone can say that he or she is in the process of creating something but few can actually say, "Here's my book." Until you have that book in your hand, the question, "Where's your book?" may be a little annoying.

In this chapter, I am going to focus on getting you inspired, your thoughts organized and your heart motivated.

Wanting to finish your book or even starting it is one thing. But taking all the steps necessary to finish that final page is quite another. Few acts take as much discipline as writing a book. The process is solitary and usually thankless. In short, you do truly have to want to do it and feel driven to do it! This, of course, begs the question "How do I get inspired?"

The single best way to get inspired is to have an idea that you love and are excited about. The more wound up you are about a given story or idea, the more you will be motivated to find the time and motivation necessary to work on your book. Simply picking an idea or a story that you aren't that thrilled about and "putting your nose to the grindstone," in order to finish it will usually prove to be a very painful process and one you should avoid.

The time you invest in finding a topic or story that truly energizes you is time very well spent. It will, in fact, save you time in the future. Thus, your first step in getting inspired is to first decide if the project you have selected actually excites you! The second step would then be to make sure that you are also excited about the plan and goals you have set. If there is anything that seems out of touch or if you have any doubts at all, then you need to step back for a second and reevaluate your plan.

Once you have a project and plan that motivates you and stirs your imagination, it is important that you do a substantial amount of research. The more information you have at your disposal regarding characters, plot points, time period, culture, ideas, clothing, historical facts and so forth, the clearer your vision will be on how to proceed. Rushing into a project simply to feel as though you are moving forward and are "now a writer" may ultimately be a hollow exercise; it is one that might even leave you feeling demoralized.

If you have a strong idea and have mapped out as many of the key details as possible, then staying inspired shouldn't be as big of a problem as you might suspect. If you have selected a strong story line and understand where you are headed with the project as a whole, then internal motivation, at least on most days, will not feel like a struggle.

Many writers looking to tackle that first book are quite concerned about where they should go for ideas. In part, this is an issue of patience and keeping an open mind. If you have a solid core concept or story and continue to play with this concept, eventually the ideas will come. Power walks can help.

It is important not to try and force the ideas to flow. The ideas will come in an organic fashion. You should set aside time to work on your book whether you are writing, organizing your ideas or brainstorming. All three of these aspects of writing should be interlinked if you want an exceptional final product.

Writing a book that is different from other books is often seen as a benchmark of its worth. Yet, being different just for the sake of being different, may not yield the results you are hoping for if it doesn't bring value to the reader. A book that is simultaneously different and authentic can be interesting and valuable. But how do you know if what you write is authentic and different? In short, this is a tough question to answer, as it is greatly dependent upon the topic, your relationship with and knowledge of this topic, and your ability to express yourself.

Regarding originality and authenticity, one of the easiest ways to chart your progress and success is research. I recommend that you invest time researching your idea or your story to see exactly how original it is. Thanks to the Internet, this process is far easier than ever before. During the research process, you might discover that your idea or story isn't quite as original as you may have hoped or you might see every reason to believe that you are on the right track.

While you can have others read your work and evaluate it for originality, its value as a creative work with something new to say may only come once it has stood the test of public scrutiny and evaluation by experts and critics. Yes, you may have to wait for time to give you this particular answer, but that is part of being a writer!

Having your work seem authentic has a great deal to do with how much of your own personality and soul you can infuse into your writing. What makes you the person you are, your experiences, your thoughts and your reactions to what you've experienced, can give readers a sense of authenticity.

Readers should feel that a genuine and fascinating person wrote the book they are reading. This level of authenticity can often make up for other shortcomings and serve to endear you to your readers as they grow to feel as though they know you. This is a benchmark of a successful writer.

Some people have a difficult time organizing their thoughts. This is a learned skill, not something you're necessarily born with, that will serve you well when beginning to write your book.

Here is a tool that I use to help me organize my thoughts on a daily basis:

Evernote: This powerful note-taking app allows you to take a photo with your phone, type in text, clip information from the Internet, use on your desktop, or use on your phone. You can download it at evernote.com or on the app store on your phone.

The best part is that it is free, although there is a paid option if you want more features. There are of course more organizational software options out there, so feel free to do your research.

I like to use Evernote because no matter where I am, as long as I have my phone I can quickly jot down ideas. It even has a recording option so if I don't want to write down the idea, then I can just speak it and play it back later.

The first thing to do to ensure your success is to write down and organize your ideas. Even if you have a photographic memory, you still need to write things down or you will eventually forget them. It takes time and energy to organize your thoughts when writing a book. We all think differently at different times of the day. There are essentially two types of thinking: specifically controlled thinking and distracted thinking.

Distracted thinking is where your mind gets easily sidetracked and lacks focus. On the other hand, controlled thinking is organized and has a purpose.

Let's look at the benefits of training your mind to think in a specifically controlled manner:

- Controlled thinking enables you to become the master of your own mind. You achieve this by learning to control your emotions and thought patterns.

- It will motivate you to work with a well-defined goal or objective.

- It supports and develops the mind as it relates to the practice of working with a clear plan.

- It improves your self-assurance.

- It allows you to arouse the subconscious mind optimistically to greater actions, in achievement of a defined objective – giving you the power you need to remove negative, damaging beliefs.

- It helps you to acquire the pattern of making correct analysis through which you can uncover solutions to your problems instead of fretting over the roadblocks you may have. The act of discovering the solutions to challenges provides peace of mind.

- It develops a creative mind rather than a lazy mind. A creative mind leads to success, where a lazy or distracted mind leads to lack of action or worse, misguided action.

- Controlled thoughts offer you a more organized life.

You might be wondering how to receive the benefits of a controlled mind. Here are five steps to consider when gaining control over your thoughts:

Think with a purpose –

What motivates you? Go get a pen and paper and write down the things that truly motivate you. When you do this you will find the purpose or the "Why" you do things. When you find what inspires you, you can move closer to the center of your thought process.

Time to concentrate –

Find a place where you can be alone for at least five minutes each day without distractions. Do not write or read during these five minutes. Simply ponder the things that you most want and need. Set goals to achieve those desires and concentrate on them without getting distracted with every little detail of how you will accomplish them. Just focus on what you desire to happen.

Get the facts –

Make use of reliable information. Facts that are connected to your purpose will help your thinking become more precise. Don't base everything you do on guesswork or hopeful wishing. There is both reliable and unreliable information on the Internet, so make sure you get your research from trustworthy sources.

Take note of all your thoughts –

If you are distracted, more than likely it is because you haven't taken the necessary time to sit down and focus on the things in your life that need to come first. When you become distracted, the first step is to realize that you are distracted. The next step, although it might sound counterproductive, is to write down what it is that is distracting you. This will help you decide whether or not what is distracting you is important in the overall scheme of things. If it's not useful, the next time the thought comes up you will be able to immediately dismiss it from your mind.

Be realistic –

Review what you write down. Organize your thoughts by grouping them into similar thoughts and showing their realistic interconnections with each other. Do this with a flexible creative mind and remember to keep it simple. You are in control of your thoughts. If you believe this and know that you have the power to decide what you want in life, then controlling your thoughts can be simple.

These five strategies are simple, but they're not easy. I say simple because most of us understand that we are in control of what we think about. But, many of us still have a hard time actually taking control. The mind is a powerful tool that when used correctly can solve any problem, overcome any obstacle and write any book.

It all comes down to self-discipline! I mean that. Up until this point, I have focused on helping you create the self-discipline you need to have before you should start writing your book. Understanding the power of self-control will help you take charge of your life. When you have self-control, the common things that have previously affected you negatively will no longer cause you to misstep. It is up to us, as individuals, to decide whether or not we are in control of our lives.

It is important for an individual to know himself inside out so that he is more fully aware of all his strengths and weaknesses. If you are certain that you have a weakness when it comes to eating too much, then you should probably put yourself in situations where you can control yourself. Furthermore, if you know that you have a hard time waking up in the morning, then writing your book in the morning probably isn't such a good strategy.

Avoid the stimulus of self-defeating behaviors. What things in your environment cause you to act in a self-destructive manner? If you recognize the factors that lead to personal disappointments such as harmful friends or a certain bar, just stay away from them. We need to be careful to make proper, self-improving decisions. So, know your weaknesses – especially those that might get in the way of you writing your book.

Self-discipline is a life-long process. Don't get down if you feel like you have a bucket full of weaknesses. Simply being aware of them will start you along the path towards unlocking the powerful person that you really are.

Now that you have a clear vision as to what you want, it is time to start the writing process. In chapters 6-8 we will be focusing all of our efforts on writing. In fact, writing is about all you will be doing, thinking about and dreaming about for the next allotted time that you committed to back in Chapters 1, 2 and 3.

Before we move on, let's do a quick recap of what we have learned in the last five chapters.

Chapter 1 – it's all about your mindset. Do you believe that you can write a book? What roadblocks are in your way and what are you going to do to overcome them?

Key ingredients to your success:

- A well devised plan/goal that you are conscious about daily
- 100% commitment to that plan/goal
- Consistent desire and follow through of your plan/goal
- MOST IMPORTANT – precise mindset

Chapter 2 – what is it that you want or need to write about? Do you feel a sense of urgency to write about the subject at hand, is it the right time? Decide how long you want your book to be.

Chapter 3 – successful writing is the result of good ideas, planning, rethinking your ideas and rewriting. How are you spending your time *before* you start writing? You must organize your time based on the results you desire.

Chapter 4 – we talked about six of the most common questions that a beginning author has.

- How and where do I start?

- In what type of style should I write my book? Simple or technical?

- How long should my book be?

- First person vs. third person?

- Can I write a book without good writing skills?

- How do I overcome writer's block?

Chapter 5 – deciding deep down where your book is. How to become inspired and stay motivated to finish. Controlled thinking vs. distracted thinking. How to develop self-control in preparation to writing your book.

Are you ready? Seriously Ready? If you are, then it's time to get started on the journey to finishing your book. With specific goals in place and a clear plan, you have everything you need to start the writing process.

Chapter 6
Forming the Core

In the last five chapters we have been through a comprehensive learning experience that if followed has given you the tools you will need to start the writing process. This chapter is going to give you insights on creating a basic map that will allow you to start writing effectively and rapidly.

Some of you may have already started writing and to you I say, "Slow Down." Why do I say this? Because you may not have created the all-important core that is essential to the writing process.

Think about the building process. Think of the creation of the Earth, a diamond, a pearl or even a house. What had to happen in order for these things to be created? There were core object(s) that initiated and/or facilitated the creation process.

Whether you believe in a higher being who created the Earth or the Big Bang Theory or something else, most will agree that there were core elements that had to be arranged prior to the Earth being formed. Without these core components, there would be no earth.

What core elements make up a diamond? Wikipedia tells us,

> "Most natural diamonds are formed at high-pressure, high-temperature conditions existing at depths of 140 to 190 kilometers (87 to 120 mi) in the Earth's mantle. Carbon-containing minerals provide the carbon source, and the growth occurs over periods from 1 billion to 3.3 billion years…"

So we learn that the core elements of a diamond are heat, pressure and carbon-containing minerals.

How are pearls created? Dolmapearl.com tells us:

> "Saltwater pearls are produced from oysters; and freshwater pearls are born from mollusks. The presence of a foreign object, like a grain of sand or a piece of shell, causes an irritation inside the oyster or mollusk. The irritation causes the secretion of nacre, which forms around the irritant, and thus creates a pearl....
>
> How long does it take to make a pearl? Freshwater pearls take much less time than saltwater pearls to form. Freshwater pearls can take between 1 and 6 years to form; whereas saltwater may take between 5 and 20 years. The longer a pearl stays in the shell, the more nacre that forms and the larger the pearl."

In the case of a pearl, the core elements are a foreign object and the accompanying organic secretion of nacre.

You could argue that there are many core elements of a house, like plumbing, electrical, framing, and so on. But the true core of a comfortable, accommodating house begins with the design and architecture. Without a design and blueprint for the house, the contractor and subcontractors wouldn't be able to create the house. They wouldn't know where to start, so they wouldn't be able to figure out how to finish.

The same is true for writing a book. Forming the core is one of the key strategies to creating a book. Without it, you will find it difficult to construct the book you desire.

Like a house, you need design, architecture and most importantly a blueprint. I will layout the four core elements of a book that will aid you in your writing process.

Here are those four important core elements in specific order.

Book Title and Subtitle
Cover (front and back)

Chapter Titles
Chapter Outlines

These are the basic components of a book. Without them, your book will lack the makeup and structure it needs.

Forming the core also gives you the blueprint necessary for you to create and write fast. Most people that I talk to and coach that have taken years to write their books or have never finished, had issues directly related to this very subject. They had no core or blueprint; therefore, they didn't know where they were going.

Don't get me wrong, if you are someone that needs a couple of years to write your book, then that is up to you and your plan and goals. It's not about how much time you take to accomplish your goals, it's about getting organized before you begin the writing process. Without a plan, we are left without a rudder and our sails are captives to the wind – taking us wherever it may.

Some of you might resist what I am about to share with you because it goes against everything you thought you knew about writing a book. But if you stay with me, I promise it will be worth it.

Let's discuss the four core elements of writing a book.

Book Title and Subtitle

The first thing that you need to do is spend some time creating the title of your book. A subtitle is optional but I like subtitles because they give you the opportunity to more intimately share your take on the subject. Fiction books rarely have them. But in my opinion, non-fiction books should always have subtitles.

I believe you should take one full day creating your title (and subtitle). This is where any research you have done (from previous chapters) will help you in the creation process. Write down anything that comes to your mind, make a whole list of titles, ask others for help and don't get discouraged if you can't think of something right off the bat.

You might be asking, "Why do I have to come up with the title before I start writing my book?"

Here is why: You are forming your core. Without a title you don't have a book. Having a title gives you encouragement, strength, and the direction you need to continue.

Keep this in mind. It doesn't matter if you don't love the title you have in front of you at the end of the day. What matters is that you have created one. You can change it after your book is finished; nothing is set in stone here. But what you will find is that the time and effort you took to think of a title and subtitle served to open your mind and shift it into the direction that you would like the book to go. This mind shift will serve you well as you sit down to write your book.

Here are some tips in helping you write your title and subtitle:

Go to Amazon.com/books and start looking at book titles. I suggest you look at all categories and genres. This will get your creative juices flowing. Spend as much time as you need. Take notes. Ponder which styles you like and that might fit your topic.

Next, focus on what you believe your book will ultimately be about. For example, my book "What Success Takes" was a somewhat simple but powerful title, or so I believed. The book is my idea on what it takes to be successful plus 30 interviews of very successful people and their stories. My second book, "The Trust Factor" is about building relationships of trust and confidence with prospects and customers to ultimately get the sale. And this book, "How To Write A Book ASAP," is all about helping first-time authors write their book fast without all of the pitfalls and roadblocks usually associated with first-time writers.

One powerful tip that can help you create your title is by doing market research – more specifically, keyword research. I have a

Forming the Core 75

training program that teaches step-by-step the process of correct keyword research. You can learn more at BuildingSocialEquity.com. If you know your market and exactly what words they are using to search online, then this may aid you in writing your title.

I'll give you a quick example. This book is titled, "How To Write A Book ASAP." That it is not an accident. I did my keyword research and found that over 33,000 people are searching this exact key phrase "How To Write A Book" in Google on a monthly basis.

I did this by going to Google's free keyword research tool. You can get there by going to **http://tinyurl.com/gkeywordtoolfree** and typing in some keywords/phrases that you think your market/niche may be searching for in the area provided at the top center of the page. Then Google will show you exactly the number of monthly searches for the specific keywords/phrases and will also give you more suggestions. This is an extremely powerful tool.

Note: Make sure you select "[Exact]" match only when doing your research on Google as shown in the following image. It is found on the middle of the screen at the left hand side of the keyword tool page.

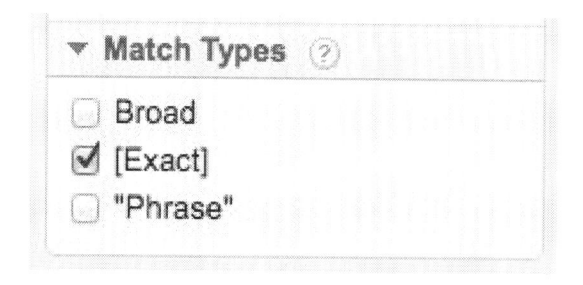

```
▼ Match Types  ⓘ
  ◻ Broad
  ☑ [Exact]
  ◻ "Phrase"
```

Your title needs to coincide with the content of your book.

Additionally, I recommend you write down in one paragraph what your book is about and for whom it is going to be written. You can practice this by telling your significant other or friend what your book is about and record what you say. Or just simply sit down and write one paragraph. No more than one paragraph or fifty words. Anything more than this will cause the exercise to become a burden.

You may come up with more than one title idea. You will need to then pick the best one and move on, remembering that you can change the title later. You will soon see another reason why the title is so important. This is where a coach or writers circle can really come in handy. Bouncing ideas off others is a huge tool for your success.

Cover (front and back)

"A picture says a thousand words." True.

"You can't judge a book by its cover." Not true!

You can judge a book by its cover; we do it all the time. You're telling me that you bought a book just because of what was inside? Not likely. Either someone told you that the book was amazing or you judged for yourself by looking at the cover, front and back.

Without a book cover, your book is incomplete. It's that simple.

You don't have to worry about a cover just yet, but you will soon realize the importance of a book's cover and how you can get one designed in chapter 7. Although we won't go into details right now, you should know that it is an important core element to your book.

Chapter Titles

Not every book has chapter titles but the majority of books do. Even if you don't want to use chapter titles in your book, you still will need divisions in your book to guide you in the writing process. They will become an integral part of your blueprint.

Chapter titles, if you choose to use them, can serve as a way to orient and control your reader's interest level and expectations. Even something as simple as "The Horrible Decision," is enough to get most readers asking, "What horrible decision? Is it really that bad? Did someone get hurt?" You get the idea. Chapter titles are easy to change, and the simple act of trying to come up with them may alter your thinking about a section of your book and send you off in a new direction. Yes, if done correctly, even deciding on chapter titles can be a mechanism to stimulate your creativity and the creative process.

Keep the chapter titles short and to the point. You aren't going to need to spend a substantial amount of time to complete this task.

If you become stuck and you feel that creating your chapter titles is taking too long, you might consider the following helpful tips.

The goal of writing a chapter title is to offer as accurately as possible the full sense of the original idea for the chapter, but in a concise, condensed form. It should state the main point, purpose, intent, and supporting details in three to eight words. You should create a title for the chapter based on what you want to share with the reader. It should correspond as a division or portion of the title of the book.

As I suggested with creating your book title, go to Amazon.com/books and search books that you have read or that catch your eye. You can then usually click on the book cover where it says, "Click to Look Inside!" In most cases you can then look at the table of contents or at some of the chapter titles. You can also grab a book off your bookshelf and start opening books and researching how other authors have written chapter titles.

Warning! Do not copy anyone's book title/subtitle or chapter titles. This is plagiarism and is illegal. Just use other books as examples and idea generators, don't copy them word for word. If you do, make sure and give the original author credit.

For those of you writing how-to books, focus on the biggest problems within the realm of your topic and book title and make those your chapter headings. A tool you can use to find out the problems in your market is by going to Google.com and searching "Forum + niche keyword(s)," here is an example:

Forum + golf

Then Google.com will more than likely find some forums you can use to research the top questions people are asking. If they aren't asking questions about the specific topic you want to cover in your book, you might want to choose a related but often discussed topic. Once you have narrowed it down you now have the ability to create chapters about those problems or questions. Back to our example of golf. Let's say the number one question is:

"What is the biggest mistake golfers make when teeing off?"

Chapter title example based from this forum question:

"Number 1 Mistake Golfers Make When Teeing Off"

If you will spend the time to research what your market needs, chapter titles will fall into place very easily.

Remember that your chapter titles can change as time goes on. They are there to support and guide you in the writing process.

Chapter Outlines

A writer should not embark on the writing of a book until he or she has a clear vision and outline of what it is he or she is going to write about or attempt to accomplish. This doesn't mean that you can't write as an exercise to sharpen your writing skills or your thought processes. But before you begin to write your book, there are many items you should already have in place.

A chapter outline gives you the ability to form a solid and coherent summary that encapsulates much of what you want to convey in that particular chapter. The importance of your outline holds true whether you are working on a fiction or non-fiction book. Without an outline, you will waste a tremendous amount of time and effort wandering around trying to get your bearings and finding your direction. When it comes to writing, not writing outlines can be a real time killer!

You may be tempted to think that the process of creating your outline is mechanical. This shouldn't be the case. When you are creating an outline, you are deciding upon what will go into your book, where and how. The chapter outline phase of your book's development is actually a highly dynamic and creative one where you are constantly making decisions, creating the story that you want to tell people and deciding what information will be included and what information will be excluded.

Regardless of whether you are writing a fiction or non-fiction work, you simply can't include "everything under the sun." Because of length guideline restrictions, you have no choice but to pick and choose information – whether it is to include what a character had for breakfast or to include a minor fact in a non-fiction work. Your outline isn't separate from your book; it is the core of your book!

During the outline phase, you will discover new paths that your argument or your characters can take, and you will find new ways of getting there. If you have chosen an outline that you like, you will be excited about working on it and watching it evolve. This, in turn, will boost your excitement when the writing phase of your book begins in earnest.

Enjoy the time that you invest during your outline phase. A strong outline will give you a solid roadmap as to where your entire project is headed. It is like an architect who sits down and designs one room at a time, making sure that the rooms all connect and that they mold to the design and blueprint intended for the entire building.

You need to understand where your project is headed, your own motivation, what you are trying to prove, as well as the motivation of your characters and what excites and depresses them. These are all elements that should at least be contemplated well before you actually sit down to begin writing your book. This is why the chapter outline is so very important. It should not be seen as somehow being separate from your book.

Understand that by writing your chapter outlines along with the book title, cover design, and chapter titles, you are simply creating a rough draft for your book. Nothing is final at this stage. Many people worry about this process because they are afraid that the amount of valuable content of their book isn't strong enough yet. Well, that may be true. But don't worry! A rough draft and a final draft are very different things.

I would like to share with you another concept that will help you write your chapter outlines. The idea is mind mapping. Creating a mind map can greatly increase the way that your mind works and creates. Mind mapping isn't for everyone so use whatever tool works best for you.

I am going to share with you, on the next page, the exact mind map and chapter outline I created for this chapter. Hopefully this will give you a good example to help you understand how my mind works.

If you can't read it, then feel free to go to www.HowToWriteABookASAP.com/mindmap

Forming the Core

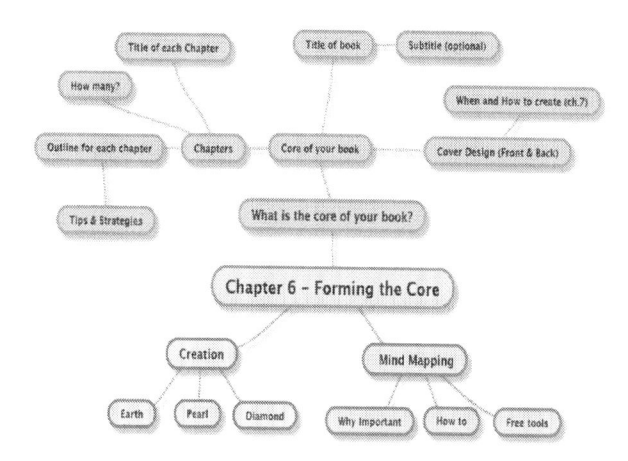

The tool that I used to create this simple mind map was the 'SimpleMind Free' app for my Macbook Pro. It was a free app that I installed on my laptop. Here is a list of other free mind mapping tools that you can use for mac or pc.

Free Mind - http://freemind.sourceforge.net/wiki/index.php/Main_Page
Bubbl.us
Mindmeister.com
TheBrain.com

Creating a mind map can support you in building your written outline. Below is the written outline for Chapter 6 that I created well in advance of writing the chapter.

    Chapter 6 Outline:

    Chapter title – Forming the Core

    Talk about the core and what the core of your book is. Talk about the creation of the earth, a diamond or pearl. It all starts somewhere.

Introduce the idea of mind mapping and show my mind map for this chapter as an example to help the reader understand the power of words and ideas.

Create in the mind of the reader what is the core of their book. Here is the core of a book in the writing process:

Title of book
Subtitle (optional)
Cover (front and back) let them know we will be covering this in detail in chapter 7
Chapter Titles
Chapter Outlines

Explain the importance of each of the above items to help the reader understand why they shouldn't just start writing, but to start with the core.

Give detailed examples of each of the above items to help the reader get ideas for their creation process.

Talk about creating chapter outlines and put this chapter outline in ch. 6 so they can see. Let them know and explain that creating outlines for a non-fiction book is different from a fictional book. Teach that research is essential.

Also let them know that nothing is set in stone and that if they spend too much time on these steps they will never begin to actually write the book, that this is just the beginning of the writing process to help them get organized.

Be sure that they know that an outline is short and sweet, not too detailed and shouldn't be more than one page, if it is then they are spending too much time and focusing too much on detail. It is just a guide and a way to get the creative juices flowing to help them start writing the chapter.

Nothing edited above, just straight from the outline that I created. Make sure that your outline is short and sweet. It shouldn't be more than one full page. Don't worry about grammar or punctuation either.

A chapter outline is simply a summary of what you plan on writing in that chapter. The process of summarizing enables you to become aware of your intent. The idea here is to effectively engage you in the creation process, allowing you to continue forming your blueprint.

While creating your chapter outline here are some things to focus on:

- Do you have the main idea and supporting details?

- Highlight the important points you plan to focus on.

- What is the purpose of the chapter?

- What is your viewpoint or the viewpoint of the character(s)?

- Ask yourself: who, what, where, when and why?

- What information do you need to gather via research?

- Arrange your information in a logical order. For example, you can start from the most to least important, in the order you see the chapter going, chronologically, by character or by scene.

- The way you organize the chapter outline may serve as a model for how you further divide and write the book.

Once you have taken all of these important, time saving and valuable steps, you can safely feel as though you are on the right path and headed in the right direction. At this stage, you have made a coherent plan and outline and you have likely improved every aspect of your book. Working on your book's core will likely give you several valuable new ideas and should increase your excitement level regarding your book as a whole.

The reason that this chapter is entitled "Forming the Core" is because everything radiates out from the core. Successful writing is a complex and layered endeavor, and that means your "core" needs to be quite strong in order to have success. Since the core is the place from which all ideas radiate, it is necessary that your core is logical, well thought out and cohesive in nature.

With all of the right information in your hands, you can now take your blueprint and beginning writing your book. Along the way you may develop a new idea that causes you to change your core element. As long as you clearly see how this will impact the rest of your chapters and the book in general, this is fine. You are, after all, an artist. As a writer, you should feel free to be inspired and react in a dynamic fashion when the opportunity for improvement arises. Your outline is not your master, but your servant. You can have that servant change roles if doing so enhances your final work.

Chapter 7

A Psychological Shift

Pick any topic or endeavor whatsoever, and chances are that at its heart is psychology. How you perceive yourself, a task or a situation is, of course, instrumental in its final outcome. Writing a book, whether it's fiction, non-fiction, a book of poetry or a collection of short stories, is the same: your attitude and belief regarding the task at hand matters a great deal.

Writing a book is a solitary act that takes patience, planning, vision, determination and, above all else, a belief in one's self. Staying motivated can be tricky, but there is no doubt about it, staying motivated is what "it" is all about. If you fail to stay motivated, you won't finish your book. Or if you do finish, it will take you years and years, and more than likely you won't be ecstatic with the final outcome. Your outlook and psychology are thus absolutely essential to being a successful writer who finishes his or her book in a timely fashion.

How can a book cover get you motivated to work on your book and finish it ASAP? Let's face it: the concept of a finished book, especially for someone who has never finished one, can seem intangible and elusive. Yet, it doesn't have to be that way. There are tricks that you can employ that will help your book seem more "real" and concrete to you. Best of all, these tricks are relatively easy and straightforward.

So how exactly can you stay motivated while working on your book? This is a topic that can be explored from a variety of perspectives, but for our purposes, we will look at a very useful motivational tool: the book cover.

When you think about your book, what do you see? More than likely you see, well, a book. But what do you see more specifically when you think about your book? You might imagine your name on the front cover. But do you imagine more? Having that tangible image fixed in your mind can help serve to motivate you to "get going" and get that book finished.

Until you are finished, your book may not seem real to you. However, if you begin the process of designing your book cover, this perception of elusiveness can change.

In fact, with a designed cover, a psychological shift occurs rapidly!

Real books have covers. When you start the process of designing your book cover, your book also will feel more real and tangible. In the process, you will find that you are infused with a new level of interest and passion about your book and about your writing.

Contemplating what your book cover may look like has other benefits as well. One major benefit is that it may actually help you sharpen aspects of your story, as you begin to think about key elements in your book. The themes revealed by this process may play a role in redefining key themes contained within your book. Either way, the process of creating your book cover can prove to be invaluable, fun and even eye-opening.

How do you go about having your book cover created. The first step is to know your title and subtitle (if applicable). We went over how to create them in the last chapter. The next step is to decide what you want your cover to look like. It is important to note that if you are unsure as to your writing topic, your goals and structure, you might not be ready to create a cover. It is one thing to use the creation of your book's cover to add clarity to your book and quite another to expect to create a book cover without a clear idea of what you are actually writing!

Once you know the fundamentals about your book, you can begin to think about which images and imagery best convey the story you wish to share with your audience. Since every book is different, there are no steadfast rules about what goes into your book. It's your book. After doing your research, you should have

A Psychological Shift

a good grasp of what themes you wish to include or keep held back.

However, unless you are also a very experienced and capable artist, odds are you won't be able to express your vision for your book cover on paper. Even if you are an accomplished artist, you may still need the advice, experience and know-how of someone who has designed book covers in the past. This calls for a dose of a powerful tool known as outsourcing.

Finding an artist to work with to help you design your book cover is a major step forward. Working with a designer on your book cover will help bring your book cover out of the realm of the imagined future and into the realm of the reality. Having a finished book cover that you can look at daily will help to keep you psychologically motivated. Just try it.

There are many ways to find a designer to help you with the design of your book cover. Thanks to the Internet, finding a book cover designer is easier and faster than ever. Of course, not just any artist will do. You need to be excited about the work and the approach that the designer takes. You must also be able to communicate effectively with the designer. Remember that the designer will need to take your words and ideas and create an appropriate book cover from them!

I am going to share with you the design company that has helped me with all of my book covers and many other website design projects. I found them at my favorite outsourcing/freelancing website, Elance.com. Their Elance.com provider name is **webxgraphics** and you can contact them at www.elance.com/s/webxgraphics

For around $100-$200 they can create an amazing book cover (front and back). Trust me; it is well worth that price, especially when you consider the motivational tool it will become.

Here are some other freelance websites:

99designs.com
Odesk.com
Guru.com

There are many designers out there that can design your cover. Here are some things that you need to focus on when searching for a designer:

- Have they created book covers before?
- Can you review their portfolio of book covers?
- How fast do they work? Can they create a mockup cover within three to five business days?
- Do they follow instructions well?
- Do they have good reviews from previous clients?
- Can you contact previous clients?
- Make sure they will give you at least 3 mockups and allow you to make changes until you are happy.

Here are three important tips in helping you communicate with your freelance designer:

Establish clear objectives. Clearly define the scope and schedule of your project. You must define your project requirements up front. Service providers want specific, comprehensive information so that they can quote you a fair, fixed price and quickly complete your job. Give vendors as much information as you can about what you need delivered and the way in which you need the work done. Also consider the idea of keeping it simple. If you try to do too much on your cover, you could confuse both the designer and the reader.

Create a wireframe. A wireframe is a model or visual representation of what you want. I do this by creating a simple word document and create a super basic book cover with all the text that I want on it. On the next page is the exact example that I shared with the designer of "How To Write A Book ASAP" book cover:

A Psychological Shift

> "You'll wonder how you ever got along without it. A powerful guide to support writing your book." – Robert Evans of the Messenger Network

How To Write A Book ASAP

The step-by-step guide to writing your first book fast!

Garrett Pierson

You can see that I showed them the exact text and layout of the book cover.

Share examples that you like. By sharing examples this gives your designer a good idea of the direction of how you would like your design to look. What I do is go to my bookshelf or Amazon.com/books and start researching books that I really like. Then I give the designer no more than three examples, my top three favorites.

The three books that I really liked and shared with the designer for this book cover were:

Strengths Finder 2.0 by Tom Rath
Great by Choice by Jim Collins
How by Dov Seidman

iStockphoto.com can be a great resource in helping you and your designer find stock photos to add to your book.

Once you give your designer these three important aspects of the project, answer any of their questions and then let them work.

Soon you will receive their first mockup. Let them know if they are at all on target. What I do is take the mockup(s) and insert them into a word document and write in text boxes the changes I want with arrows to specific areas on the design (I insert arrows using the 'insert' and shapes' tabs in Microsoft Word).

Visit **HowtowriteabookASAP.com/mockups-1** to see the first two mockups the designer provided.

Then visit **HowtowriteabookASAP.com/mockups-2** to see the next design mockups after I sent requested changes to the designer.

Now visit **HowtowriteabookASAP.com/final** to see the final design cover.

Imagine how I felt when I started receiving those mockups and then when I finally received my final book cover. Do you think it motivated me to finish the book? You better believe it!

You won't know what I mean until you actually try it yourself. What do you have to lose?

You might be wondering about the back cover of the book.

I usually wait until I have finished the book to have the back cover created. Also, I use the same designer that created my front cover to do the back cover. If you feel that your designers are on a roll with the front cover, feel free to have them complete the back cover as well. But REMEMBER that as you are getting the cover designed that you need to be writing too, don't let the cover get in the way of your progress, it is simply a motivational tool.

The back cover usually includes the following items:

A short description of the contents of the book. This description needs to be very compelling to get the reader interested in your book. I suggest the book, "Words That Sell" by Richard Bayan to help you with your back cover description. Bullet points are also very good. For a novel you might want to include in your description information about a character.

Endorsements and/or Testimonials. This gives the reader social proof that you are an authority or that the book is worth reading. This is just a suggestion. If you can't get endorsements or testimonials from well-respected associates by the time you print, you can add these onto the second printing of your book.

'About the Author' area. The back cover could include a short bio and photo of you as the author.

ISBN and Barcode. When designing the back cover, keep in mind to free up the space needed for an ISBN and Barcode if you plan on selling the book. In my full author-training program I teach the step-by-step process of getting these numbers and codes. You can find out more about my program at HowToWriteABookASAP.com/training

How you want to design your book covers, both front and back, are exclusively your decision unless you are working with a publisher. But whether you use your original cover or one that has changed substantially from your first try, having the book come to life for you through the cover early on in the writing process will continue to motivate you day after day.

Creating your book cover can help you achieve the psychological shift you need. Any tool that can help motivate you and keep you motivated is one that you should fully embrace! There are many tools to increase your motivation and keep you writing, but the tool of creating your book's cover and keeping it in front of you as you write is one of the best visualization tools you will find.

Chapter 8
Write NOW!

By this stage of the game, you should be motivated and well on your way to writing your book. By the time you reach this chapter, you should have created a coherent outline, you should know who your characters are and understand their motivations. And you should know where "it's all going." But if you don't know these things, does that mean you should give up? Of course not!

We have discussed the steps you need to take to prepare to write and to stay motivated. We have gone over the importance of creating your book cover as a visual tool and aid for helping you stay motivated. Armed with all of this information, you should be well on your way to consistently writing and gradually making your way towards your ultimate goal. If you are not incrementally reaching your goal of finishing your book, it is important that you stop what you are doing, whatever it may be, and ask yourself, "Why am I not writing more? Why am I not making more progress?" The answer to these questions may be obvious, or they may be more hidden from your view – even subconscious. Regardless, if you are not reaching your goal, you have to work to resolve the issue.

You may discover that you need to retrace your steps and rework your outline so that your characters and/or content are more "flushed out." Or you may find that your story or premise is not as strong as you would have liked. The process of writing is one of discovery and evolution. Embrace this as a fact and your writing will benefit as a result.

Every day you should be setting aside time to write. If you have all your ideas in order, you are clear on key story elements and have completed your research, then it's time to move forward. If you are finding it difficult to set aside some time every day to write, then you must find out why. Go back to Chapter 3 for more help on organizing your time.

Oftentimes, distractions will keep you from writing when you have planned to write. Being dedicated to finishing your book means that you will find the time to write today and tomorrow until you eventually finish; so get dedicated. Yes, it is actually that simple, and you need to see it that way as well! Finishing your book is a systematic process.

If at any point you find yourself suffering from writer's block, just step back for perspective. Ask yourself deep and exploring questions about your characters. Who are they and why do they behave the way that they do? How do they interact with those around them? How do they see the world? Why should your readers love them or hate them or feel indifferently or confused by them or their behavior? Try and view your work from the audience's point of view. What kind of questions would you like to see addressed or answered if you were reading the book you are writing? How would you feel about the various characters that populate your written world?

If you are writing non-fiction, stop and ask yourself if your argument is logical and coherent. Step back and examine your argument for flaws and weaknesses. Are there any key points or important insights that you are ignoring? These questions can all act as simple but effective tools for reshaping your thinking towards your work and, in the process, help you break free from any potential writer's block.

Writing isn't simply about putting words on a page. It's about creating a mood, tone and feel that leaves readers reacting as though they were impacted in some fashion. The reader should feel that they experienced something new and educational, comical, or uplifting. Often readers have trouble pinning down exactly what it was about a book that they liked so much. It is quite the accomplishment for writers when this takes place. This means the reader has created the story in their minds and has filled in any gaps you may have left out, even if it was on purpose.

Have you ever seen a movie that was based on a novel? Did you like the movie much less than you liked the book? Why? I think it is because when you were reading the book you were imagining and role playing it in your mind. That's why the movie couldn't compare to the book; the story was altered by how you had imagined it.

Writing a book is a process. This fact is pointed out with great frequency especially in writing classes. Yet, in the "heat of battle" where words hit the page, many writers fail to remember this reality.

Nothing is better than being on a roll. Yet when that rolls ends, make sure you step back and look at what you have written with fresh eyes. Sometimes this means that you will need the perspective only time can bring. You must continue writing even if you feel that you need to fix something. We've talked about this before but I want to engrain it deeper in your mind. Do not stop writing to edit! Just write. Understand the process and accept the fact that you can fix the grammar, punctuation and spelling errors later. After you're done writing, you can go back and review what you have written. And even if you're an English professor by trade, your copy editor needs to make the final revisions.

A large part of the writing process is embracing the fact that you simply must review and revise your work in order to improve it. Remember that when you rewrite your text, it doesn't mean that you failed the first time. Don't get into a negative frame of mind. Instead, look at rewriting as a valuable process that gradually improves what you have accomplished, kind of like hitting a home run instead of a single. Nothing is wrong with hitting a single. Those who know me well know that I love the game of baseball. I have spent thousands of hours swinging the bat. And just like any other player, I would be happy with hitting a single every time I step up to the plate. What I am trying to teach here is that you shouldn't stop writing mid-swing to edit your book. Let the creative juices keep flowing as long as possible. Realize that your first draft is going to be a single and accept it. Pete Rose made a career out of base hits, doing it 4,256 times and relying on his skill at stealing bases and the hitting skills of his teammates to help him score.

When you review and revise what you have written – after you've completed your first draft, you can steal a base or two, turning that single into a double or triple depending on your editing skills. Then your editor, as a key, skilled member of your team, will help you score. Editing your book personally and then professionally gives you the ability to stop time, as it were. It allows you to see exactly where the ball will be when it crosses the plate, how fast it is coming and at what angle, so that when you're finished with the book you'll have knocked it out of the park!

It is also important to know when you have edited your book sufficiently and it's time to hand it off to a professional editor. Just like in baseball, if you try to swing too hard, chances are you'll strike out. There is a fine line between hitting a home run and striking out. Babe Ruth had 1,330 strike outs compared to 714 home runs. This fear of striking out is perhaps why only a small percentage of the population attempts to write a book in the first place and why an even smaller percentage actually finishes.

By focusing every day and telling yourself "I am going to write NOW!" it will happen; you will finish your book on schedule and you will be happy that you did.

I now would like to focus on some ideas to help you write your book. I have made it pretty obvious that to finish your book you have to write, but I haven't given you many strategies on how to write.

Your writing will come from personal experiences in your life, much like I have in sharing my love of baseball, for example.

This is what will make your book unique and authentic. It's what will endear your readers to you. Accept inspiration from within and pull from emotions you currently have and those you have felt in the past. Here is a list of emotions that might help you when you're writing:
http://en.wikipedia.org/wiki/List_of_emotions.

Express yourself and let go of what's inside without letting up. The emotions and expressions will flow through you into words. All you have to do is organize them into stories and concepts to entertain and help the reader.

There are several different methods that you can use to write your book, which are:

Typewriter – old school
Paper and Pen/Pencil – good luck
Illustrated – children or miscellaneous
Computer – 21st century
Spoken/Recorded – new age

Ninety-percent of you will likely write your book with word processing software on your computers. Don't worry about what type of software to use. Just write! But I do want to share with you a way for you to write your book faster than you could ever imagine. Let me explain.

It should come as no surprise that most people are more comfortable with talking than they are with writing. Your brain is wired to allow you to speak in an easy and free flowing way. After all, as discussed in a previous chapter, you have been speaking and expressing your thoughts verbally since you were just a baby. However, when you try to put words on paper, the brain often stutters. As a result, the writing process tends to be nowhere near as fluid as when we speak.

So why not speak your book?

This is exactly how I wrote my first book "What Success Takes." I bought a microphone and some recording software for my laptop and simply spoke my book. When I say that I spoke my book, I mean that I sat in front of my recorder, started talking in a formulated way and the recordings later became written words through transcription.

Note: This is not for everyone, but it may work for you.

Here are the steps and tools to speaking your book:

Step 1: Purchase a recording device or use one that is built into your computer. I purchased an Audio Technica USB Mic (Model AT2020), because I wanted great quality so I could turn the book into an audio book to go along with the printed version. But you can use anything that records your voice; you don't have to spend a lot of money.

Step 2: Find recording software (only needed if using a microphone for your computer). I used free software called Audacity that you can download at Audacity.sourceforge.net

Step 3: Record. Important tip – make sure the audio is recording, test thoroughly.

Step 4: Edit your recording with the software you chose above.

Step 5: Send the recorded files to a transcriber. As mentioned earlier, I used Tamara Bentzur who is fast, reliable and accurate! You can find her here - tbentzur.wordpress.com

Step 6: After you have reviewed and revised the transcriptions, send them to your copy editor for editing. (We'll discuss more about copy editors in Chapter 9)

That is basically it. The amazing thing is now you have audio and written word. You can package your book with two channels of distribution instead of one.

From my testing, I have found that if you talk at a semi-fast pace for around seven to fifteen minutes you can easily create on average about six pages of written content for a 5.5 x 8.5 inch book. Think of that. All you have to do is speak your book for around fifteen minutes a day and you could easily write a two hundred-page book in eight to ten hours.

I must repeat myself in saying that recording your book is not for everyone. It is simply a suggestion that you might not have thought of before. My last two books have both been written with word processing software on my laptop and not spoken. However, my next book will be spoken. I don't really have a preference as I have enjoyed both approaches.

When writing your book with a computer you have a couple options:

- PC or Mac

- Laptop or Desktop

- Microsoft Word, Pages, Notepad, Wordpad, Textedit, Wordperfect, Openoffice, Google Docs, Evernote and so on

- Blogging Platforms – Wordpress, Blogger, Movable Type, and so on

- Professional Writing software – top ten here: creative-writing-software-review.toptenreviews.com

For me the choice was easy. I write in Microsoft Word on a Macbook Pro.

At the end of the day it really comes down to either writing or speaking although if you really feel more comfortable writing it by hand, (I know this applies to a few of you) there are transcribers available to type it when you're done. If you get too caught up in the software or tools then you are taking time away from what is important: WRITING!

If you talk to any writer, editor or publisher they will give you different and varying ideas of how a book should be written. Almost everyone has their own unique idea of the most effective writing process.

It ultimately comes down to these five main points:

1. A Congruent Beginning, Middle and End
2. A Main Idea
3. Effective Description Incorporating Emotion
4. A Well-defined and Meaningful Purpose/Plot
5. Consistent Tone and Flow

Reread those. That is writing summed up. In most cases, it doesn't matter if the writing is a non-fiction, fiction, essay, press release, blog post, or anything else that you are writing.

Let me be very honest. If you want rules and guidelines on how to write your book then there are thousands of empty articles on the subject that seem to all be relative. You can research them until your brain goes numb. Point being that you just need to start writing and let your knowledge, experiences and inspiration do the work. If you worry too much about the "How," the likelihood of you finishing your book is slim to none.

If you want to write a novel, I suggest Jeff Gerke's course that you can access here – HowToWriteABookASAP.com/novel-course

If you want an effective way to write a non-fiction book then I suggest my training course. You can learn more about it here – HowToWriteABookASAP.com/non-fiction-course

Investing in a coach or mentor that has done what you want to do can provide you with the confidence and tools you need to succeed. It doesn't matter whether it is weight loss or writing a book, a mentor gives you power to effectively guide you through the process in an orderly, time-saving fashion because of their experience. In short, you have nothing to lose and everything to gain by investing in a writing coach or mentor.

One last tip.

We have touched on this before, but we need to recap the importance of your writing environment. This includes everything from sleeping, eating and exercise habits to the inspiration-inducing room in which you write.

Interestingly enough, I am currently writing this chapter in a room that is cold. My feet are cold and I am a bit tired. This is affecting the effectiveness of my writing and how I am able to engage myself to be as productive and creative as possible. So I might move into a different room or put on warmer clothes. I may even stop writing for a while and come back later.

As you schedule a time to write, be specific in where you will write as well, how much sleep you will get, and what you will eat and drink. Some people write better with a cup of coffee being constantly refilled. Others write with music playing in the background. If you haven't already, you will soon find what creates and helps maintain an atmosphere conducive to the inspiration you need and what doesn't.

Your location and mindset will not only affect the way you write. It will also affect how fast you write. All I am asking is that you be aware.

Chapter 9

The Publishing Fairytale

Writing a book may not be the easiest thing you ever do, but it will certainly be one of the more rewarding and self-fulfilling things that you take on. By writing a book, you have told yourself and the world at large something about you. Namely, you have told the world that you can start something large, perhaps even monumental, and finish it. After all, how many people actually set out to write a book and never get it done?

How is your book coming? Do you have a rough draft?

Finishing your book is, in many respects, only the beginning. You might not want to think about this while you are still trying to put relevant words down on the page. But the fact is that once you have written the book, you have to ask yourself, "What's next?"

It's now time to decide the route you are going to take for getting your book published. There are only two ways to accomplish this:

Traditional publishing or self-publishing.

A publisher and literary agent will sell you on traditional publishing (even though traditional publishing is changing rapidly and there are many names for it). I have nothing against this channel. I do, however, recommend the self-publishing route.

Once upon a time, the only way to reach large numbers of people was through literary agents and book publishers. However, the world of the Internet has changed this equation significantly. Gone are the days when you must funnel your work through self-appointed gatekeepers who decide what is exceptional, good, average and horrible. Of course, this hasn't exactly made the gatekeepers happy, but that isn't your problem. Your challenge is to optimize your time and effort, making the most effective decisions that will get your book seen by as many people as possible.

Is it too harsh to call believing in the world of publishing a "fairytale?" Not really! When you step back and analyze the number of books that are submitted to agents and publishing houses versus the number of books actually published, you quickly realize that the odds of getting published are extremely low, especially if it is your first book. Publishers are looking to maximize profits. All one has to do is look at the kind of books that are being published to realize that the concept of "literature" and "art" have mostly been abandoned by the traditional publishing industry in favor of 'what sells.'

If you doubt this, take a trip to your local big box bookstore and see what you are offered. You will find books from celebrities, fluffy books on pop culture with the majority of shelf space taken up by authors who are really industries unto themselves. Yes, we are looking at you, Stephen King, as well as countless others.

In most cases, those looking to break into the publishing industry must have a pretty exceptional "in" if he or she is to be one of the few chosen to have their book published. Today, you either need a very unique angle or an existing platform that will help promote the book or you simply need to know someone. Unfortunately, it really is that simple. Believing otherwise is like believing in a fairytale without any realistic chance of a happy ending!

So, what are you to do if you want to live your dream and become a published author? First, don't waste your time with publishers and agents. Even if you do get a publisher's interest, there is no guarantee that this publisher will effectively promote your book or even print very many copies. Then there is the all-important issue of money!

The Publishing Fairytale

Even if you do get a publisher, that doesn't mean you are going to get a massive payday. Most authors will need a literary agent, and you can expect that agent to take at least 10% of your revenue. Some ask for much more. Of course, this varies widely and wildly from publisher to publisher and from agent to agent. Authors can expect to earn royalties of perhaps 10% of the retail price. In short, it's a shark eat shark business.

Here is a small look into the traditional publishing process (by scribendi.com, an unbiased source):

> "In traditional publishing, the author completes his or her manuscript, writes a query letter or a proposal, and submits these documents to a publishing house (or has a literary agent do this for them, if one can be acquired). An editor reads it, considers whether it is right for the house, and decides either to reject it (leaving the author free to offer it to another publisher) or to publish it. If the publishing house decides to publish the book, the house buys the rights from the writer and pays him or her an advance on future royalties. The house puts up the money to design and package the book, prints as many copies of the book as it thinks will sell, markets the book, and finally distributes the finished book to the public…
>
> … With traditional publishing, a manuscript can take years to become a book. First, an author may have to pitch the manuscript to several publishing houses before it is picked up. Considering that the bigger houses can take up to six months to work through the "slush pile" (the multitude of queries on editors' desks) to get to your manuscript and that you will likely have to try several publishing houses before you get one to show interest…well, you do the math! That's a lot of waiting. Then, if a house does decide to take your book, the actual process of producing the book takes at least another year. Admittedly, this process applies mainly to fiction. Nonfiction books that are topical and relevant to

current world events might be pushed through more quickly."

Personally, traditional publishing isn't my cup of tea. I have never gone that route. But if you want to go this route, good luck. If a publishing company comes to you and they want to publish your book, then I suggest you do it. I have friends and colleagues that are publishers and they do a great job. Because this is my book, I have chosen to steer you away from the challenges of established publishing houses. You can do what you want with your book. Just remember that if you publish with a traditional publisher, it becomes their book depending on how the contract is set up, so be careful.

For those of you who want to go the route of traditional publishing, I totally understand. In fact, in my training course, I have numerous resources and interviews with traditional publishers that will provide you with additional insight.

However, you should know that:

> "Many famous authors and their books were rejected multiple times. Publishers turned down Richard Bach's Johnathan Livingston Seagull no less than 140 times; Margaret Mitchell's Gone With the Wind received 38 "no's," while Stephen King's Carrie was turned down 30 times. J. K. Rowling's original work was pooh-poohed by 12 publishers…guess who's kicking themselves now that they passed on Harry Potter? And E. E. Cummings first work—*The Enormous Room,* now considered a masterpiece—was ultimately self-published…and dedicated to the 15 publishers who rejected it." - selfpublishingresources.com

Time to move on to the other option: self-publishing.

Self-publishing is a lot of work and carries with it a fairly substantial learning curve. But you have a much, much greater chance of reaching your audience through this means than by trying to chase down the publishing fairytale.

Thanks to the Internet, e-books are valuable alternatives to written books, making it possible for a new author to reach people directly without the gatekeepers and middlemen. Blogs, online radio shows and ecommerce sites that specialize in selling books and tools as well as social media can also assist in the distribution of the written word.

Is this a revolution? It most definitely is!

Those who are willing to put the time and effort into self-promotion have a good chance at being rewarded both financially and emotionally by having their book available to the masses. In Chapter 10, I am going to share with you ways that you can make additional income with your book. So don't skip the last chapter.

In teaching you how to self-publish your book, I am going to share with you the exact steps that I have taken to self-publish my books. Pay close attention.

Step 1: Write the book.

Ok, that's pretty obvious but it's the truth. You shouldn't even worry about steps 2-9 until you have at least written a rough draft.

Step 2: Find a proofreader.

This can be your mom, grandpa, friend or milkman. You need someone that has some type of reading and English (or your language) skills. If you can find someone you can trust who is familiar with the topic or industry that will give you honest feedback, that's productive too. While they are reading the book, have them take notes. When they are done reading, ask them to let you know which areas of your book need to be rewritten or revised.

Make sure that they know you are looking for constructive criticism and then be willing to accept it. A friend who says "That looks great!" without changing a thing shouldn't be used as a proofreader. Also make sure that they can do this in a short amount of time. Give them a date to finish by or you could be waiting forever.

Step 3: Rewrite if needed.

Make sure you are willing to read through your work and make any necessary changes. Add dialogue, delete unimportant details, and reword paragraphs. Keep in mind that you still aren't worrying much about grammar, punctuation and spelling at this point.

Step 4: Hire a copy editor.

This is where you need to start focusing on all the grammatical mistakes in your writings. I suggest you outsource this to a professional. There are many professional copy editors out there that will edit your book for a fee.

I use Aaron Brandley as my copy editor and recommend him with the utmost respect. You can contact him at aaron@ArticlesandSubmissions.com. Aaron turns on "Track Changes" under the "Review" tab in Microsoft Word before ripping apart my books. This allows me to see all the changes and accept or reject them as I see fit (most of the time I accept his changes).

Those of you who have had nightmares about writing an unreadable book, have no fear. Copy editors like Aaron can take your words and make them sing! As this is by far your most expensive investment in the writing of your book, be sure you find a copy editor who you trust will work hard to make you look good.

As it is my goal to be completely transparent with you, here is one example of how Aaron edited one paragraph of this book:

My draft:
"Finishing" your book is, in many respects, only the beginning. This might be hard to think about when you are still in the process of trying to get words down on page, but the fact is that once you have a book on file, you have to ask yourself, "what next?"

His edited version:
Finishing your book is, in many respects, only the beginning. You might not want to think about this while you are still trying to put relevant words down on the page. But the fact is that once you have written the book, you have to ask yourself, "What's next?"

Aaron also does ghost writing (where the author tells him the story and he writes it) and writes quality articles for online companies and then manually submits them to social media and article directory sites for increased circulation.

You can also find freelance copy editors online. I suggest Elance.com, Odesk.com or Guru.com. Make sure that you look for good reviews and that you make contact with previous customers before hiring someone. Also make sure that they can edit your book in a timely manner.

Step 5: Create additional pages.

Once you have received the final edited version of your book it is time to create the following additional pages:

Title cover
Copyright page
Table of contents

All the rest are optional:
About the author

List of figures
List of tables
Dedication
Acknowledgments
Foreword
Preface
Introduction
Appendix
Glossary
Index
Notes
Bibliography

Step 6: Find a printer.

There are many options when it comes to finding a book printing company. I will share only a couple.

My favorite is 48hrbooks.com. I have used them for all my books. They are fast and very affordable. The only problem with this method is that you will have to keep the inventory at your house or office.

The following companies I personally have never used, so you are going to have to do your own research.

LuLu.com has POD (Print on Demand) options that you may want to look into.

CreateSpace.com, formally Booksurge, was acquired by Amazon.com and is another very popular option.

AuthorHouse is another great option for writers that want a one-stop-shop for self-publishing. Find out more at Authorhouse.com/ServicesStore/ChoosePackage.asp

Step 7: Get an ISBN number and barcode.

If you want to sell your book then you are going to need an ISBN number and barcode. The process is very simple and the place that you can get an ISBN number and barcode for a printed book or an e-Book is at ISBN.org, which will lead you to Myidentifiers.com.

Step 8: Hire a typesetter.

Again, I suggest you outsource this to a professional. Typesetting is a process that gets your book ready for the printer. For example if you want a 5.5 x 8.5 inch book then you need to format the written word to fit the required measurements. A professional typesetter knows exactly how to accomplish this task.

For my typesetting I use Susan A. She can be found at Elance.com/s/carlshaven/.

Step 9: Finalize cover design (front, back and spine).

In Chapter 7 we discussed starting the process of designing your book's cover. If necessary, go back to that chapter to reference the importance of the book cover and how to create one.

Now it's time to create the back cover (refer to Chapter 7 for back cover ideas) and spine for your book.

Note that in order to have the correct size for the spine you will need to know the exact number of pages that your book has once you have received the final back from your typesetter.

For all of my books I have used John from Speedread, an Elance.com provider. You can find him at www.elance.com/s/speedread. I turn my book cover designs (front and back) over to them and they create the spine and everything else required to submit the cover to the printer. I don't worry about the details. As is the case for all of the people I use for my outsourcing needs, they know what they're doing. Keep in mind that all of the service providers that I have mentioned in this book are willing to accept work, but have the choice to turn anyone down if they are too busy.

Step 10: Submit all required files to printer.

If you have followed the previous steps, then you should have everything ready for the printer. Make sure that you follow their requirements so that you can submit everything needed in an orderly fashion. This will save you a lot of headaches and money. If they have to make any changes to your files then this will come out of your pocket.

I usually ask for a final proof (PDF file) and I also opt for a printed proof before the book goes to full print. This gives me the opportunity to see what the book will look like and make any final changes.

I get a lot of people that ask me how much self-publishing costs. So let me break down every expense for me to print off 100 books.

Book cover - $150 (front and back) + $75 for spine and formatting. Total = $225
Proofreading/Copy editing = $1500 (for about 120+ page book)
Typesetter = $100
ISBN & Barcode = $150
100 Printed Books + Printed Proof and Shipping = $500 (varies based on book size, page numbers, color pages and printer)

Total cost = $2,475 and worth every penny.

Keep in mind that $1,975 of the $2,475 total are one-time expenses. After those, you will only have to pay for any additional printed books. Your costs will vary based on the providers and printer that you use.

Another option you have is to start out with an e-Book version of your book. You may find this more affordable and simple to begin your journey as a self-published author.

An e-Book is a electronic version of your book that can be read by various types of online, mobile and e-Book reader devices, including iPad, Amazon Kindle/Fire, Kobo eReader, Nook, etc.

Here are just a few amazingly insightful quotes to help you understand the importance of the e-Book market:

> "I expect e-books to be the fastest-growing segment that publishing has ever seen." – Brian Murray, CEO of Harper Collins

> "Publishers need to take digital seriously, they must make it the new default for publishing, preparing for a day in which physical book publishing is an adjunct activity that supports the digital publishing business." – James McQuivey, Forrester Research

> "There are dozens of "indie" authors who are selling thousands of e-books a month without a print version." – Simon Owens, thenextweb.com

> "If [publishers] wanted my three-book vampire series, a quarter of a million dollars wouldn't even do it, because I can make more than that in a year on those three books." – Tina Folsom, Self-published author selling e-books

> "Since April 1, 2011 Amazon sold 105 books for its Kindle e-reader for every 100 hardcover and paperback books, including books without Kindle versions and excluding free e-books." – NYTimes.com

I could go on and on with quotes and stats showing the potential success that authors can have with e-books. I won't, mainly because the numbers are increasing and changing so rapidly that I would have to change this book monthly. Just trust me when I say that you are missing out on millions of potential readers if you don't have an e-book version of your book available.

It is important to know that there are several different formats that you will need to create in order to reach all the e-book markets.

Here are the major e-book retailers: **Amazon, Apple, B&N, Sony, Ingram, and Kobo.**

Here are just some of the different formats needed to submit to the major retailers:
Epub, Mobi, PDF, PDB, TXT

eBookit is a company that I use to format my e-book for me and submit to all the major e-book retailers – ebookit.com/orderIt costs only $149 and they do everything for you, and I mean everything. In fact they even give you an e-book ISBN number. WOW!

Let's conclude the chapter. Are there pros and cons to both traditional publishing and self-publishing? Yes. Can I tell you which one is best for you? No. It is up to you and your decision depends upon your strategy.

It doesn't necessarily matter the path that you take, what matters is that you print the book you have spent so much time and energy to create. Even if you only print ten copies, you will feel the pleasure of accomplishment and fully experience the power and authority that comes from being able to say that you are an author.

This chapter could bring up various concerns or questions all of which can be answered at HowToWriteABookASAP.com/questions. Also, be sure to take advantage of my step-by-step online training course if you haven't done so already. I go into much more detail on how to self-publish or publish your book.

Chapter 10

Book's Done! What's Next?

Do you want to know what is scarier than the thought of sitting down and writing a book? Not knowing what to do once you are done!

Once you have written a book, rewritten it again, had it checked for spelling, structure and grammatical issues, developed a book cover and published the book, then what? This can be the most terrifying question that a first time author can ask. You should realize that as terrifying as this question may be, doing nothing is a far scarier proposition.

Finishing a book is a Herculean task. This fact is especially true if you took the process seriously and created a new world with characters that you care about. Seeing your book "sit there" unread, unappreciated and uncared for is a heartbreaking experience and one that you want to avoid. Thus, you don't want to look at your book as being "finished" until everyone in the world knows about it. Maybe you'll never have a best seller that is in the hands of millions. Maybe you'll never have the hottest star or even a washed up, aging actor playing the lead in the movie based on your book. But there are steps you can take to get people to read it.

Getting your book recognized is vital, for it can lead to more books. This means you get to do more of what you love, namely, creating through the process of writing. If you only remember one detail from this book, it should be to realize that just because you have written the "last word," your task is not over. Hopefully, your connection with your book will never die, as readers will always be asking you questions about it. If you don't get the immediate response you had hoped for, don't give up on it – not at least until you have explored every avenue that you can think of and then some!

Remember that even if you get your book published the traditional way, in most cases, the publishing house is going to do very little to actually market your book. Even in a great economy, they will do the minimum expected of them. In a bad economy you can be sure that they will print your book, distribute it, and quit. So, no matter what publishing platform you use, you are going to have to market your book.

Some of you might be reading this and be thinking to yourself, "I am not a marketer and I don't want to be one." In this case you have two options:

Outsource the marketing or figure it out.

Of course outsourcing won't be cheap. The other option of figuring it out is going to take time to learn but your newly gained knowledge will be worth it in the long run.

This chapter is going to give you a kick start into the marketing process of your book. Keep in mind that what I have included in this book is just a small sample of what I can teach you. Within my online course "How To Write A Book ASAP," you get access to my full Building Social Equity 2.0 training course that teaches more in-depth online marketing from Search Engine Optimization and Social Media to Video Marketing. This course alone is worth over $497. However, if you are already a member of the "How To Write A Book ASAP" online training course then you already have full instant access. Otherwise, make sure you check out how to access the course and bonus courses at HowToWriteABookASAP.com/training.

So, what do you do once you've penned that last word on the last page and the book is published? First, take time to realize that you have accomplished something great and fantastic. For this achievement, you deserve a pat on the back. Even those who have written truly awful books with a capital "A" merit recognition. The fact that they finished them says a great deal about their dedication, persistence and goal-driven organizational skills. Your book, on the other hand, because of your preparation and inner-motivation is going to be incredible!

Regardless of what kind of book you have written and what resources you have at your disposal, there are additional steps you can take after your book has been written to get it out to the world.

Online outlets exist where you can both promote and sell your book. This opportunity was unheard of just a few years ago. Now, for the first time in history, it is possible for works that would have never seen the "light of day" instead reach an extensive audience. As a writer, you want your work to be seen and read.

The Internet tools that are making the World Wide Web so exciting are often the exact same tools that writers can utilize to help promote their books. The Internet is full of tools designed specifically to help people promote their products and services. And you, as a new author, can take advantage of this myriad of valuable tools. Whether we are talking about Facebook, Twitter, YouTube or a range of other sites, you can effectively promote yourself in numerous ways.

Keep in mind that no matter what kind of book you wrote, there will always be an audience for it. The audience may vary in size and level of enthusiasm, but it is out there! For example, if you wrote Western fiction, there are independent websites and blogs dedicated to all things Western that will likely give you coverage and attention. Just ask! You can also find forums and groups on sites such as Facebook that will be interested in the kind of book you have written.

By being proactive and marketing your book via all the online paths currently available to you, it is possible to have countless people read excerpts, summaries and entire chapters of your book. I even suggest giving your book away for free.

"Are you kidding me? Give my book away for free?" you say!

Sure, why not!

If you give your book away for free to someone who really appreciates it, you can build a loyal following, and you'll be able to sell even more of them later.

Take a look at the diagram below:

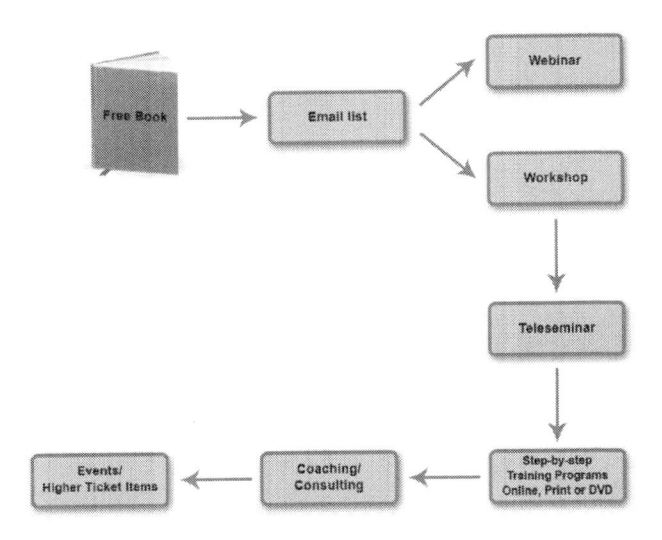

In this example, in order for someone to get the book for free they have to enter their email address and agree to receive emails from you (they can unsubscribe whenever they want).

Then, from the email list, you build a relationship with this person and invite them to online webinars, workshops or teleseminars. Then you sell them step-by-step training programs – online, print or DVD.

You can then offer coaching/consulting worth thousands of dollars.

And going even further you can create live events or even higher ticket items. You can write a second book and sell it to people who received your first book for free.

For those of you who wrote a novel, it might look like this:

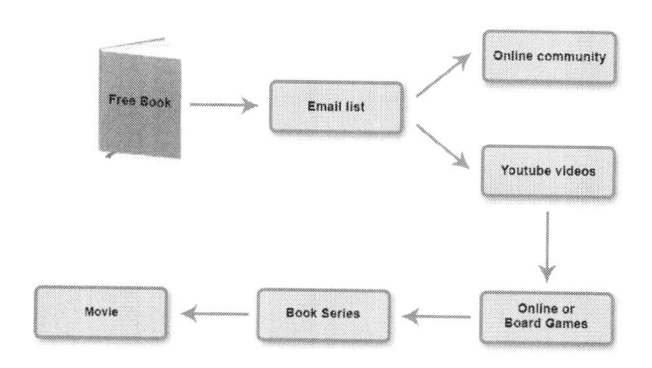

```
Free Book ──→ Email list ──→ Online community
                         ──→ Youtube videos
                                   │
                                   ↓
Movie ←── Book Series ←── Online or Board Games
```

You give the book away and create a huge fan base. You can create an online community to let the readers communicate and add to your story or create viral Youtube.com videos.

Then you could create an online game or board game or character figures that people can purchase.

You would then write more books that are sequels or prequels to your original book and offer them all as a series.

The ultimate payout would be with a movie based on your novel.

There really are boundless ideas and opportunities that you can come up with when going the free route; these are just a few suggestions.

I know that some of you will think I am crazy with the idea of giving a book away for free, but consider this; you don't have to give the print version away for free. Why not just give the electronic version away? This is also known as an e-book. This way there would be almost no cost to you as the author. It is a viable option capable of creating a fan base who will become loyal to you even as a first-time author.

Bottom line: If you want a greater chance at building a solid, ongoing relationship of trust with your readers, you need to establish yourself as a credible, trusted authority in your market. The more enthusiastic readers you have, the more credible you will become.

One thing to keep in mind is the word 'building' in the phrase "building a relationship of trust." It usually takes time to establish credibility and trust with a reader, which means that you have to try to engage them through more than one type of medium. With that in mind, here are ten ways that you can keep your followers' interest while building an interactive relationship with them:

- Email Marketing
- Webinars
- Teleseminars
- Social Media
- Direct Mail
- Magazine
- Podcasts
- Applications
- Live Streaming Video
- Live Events

You will need to decide which of these methods to use based on which will work best for you and your niche. You don't have to implement all of these strategies, but I do suggest that you apply at least two.

EMAIL MARKETING

Let's take a look at why email marketing is so effective when building relationships.

- **Email marketing is highly scalable.** By composing an email and customizing it to suit the reader, with the click of a button you can reach thousands of people instantly! Unlike an 'offline' business where the more customers you have, the busier you are, in email marketing, it is much easier. Regardless of the size of your mailing list, whether it is 100 or 10,000, your entire email list gets notified – all with the same amount of effort!

- **Email marketing is personal.** Auto-responders allow you to customize the emails, allowing you to connect with the subscriber individually. The more personalized your email, the better the result (so treat it as though you are writing to your best friend).

- **You can automate many tasks with your auto-responder.** For every new opt-in subscriber, you can schedule your emails, building a unique relationship with them. You can choose what to send to them, when to send it to them and the frequency between each email.

- **Email marketing acts as a good pre-sell.** You might not be able to cram a sales letter into your email, but at least you can pre-sell your subscriber and lead a subscriber to your blog, sales letter or website to check out what you have to offer. Test out different ways that will put them in the right frame of mind before they evaluate what you have to offer.

- **Email also works well to sell more.** Once they have received your book and they like it, there is a good chance they'll be interested in more.

Whether you are emailing your subscribers daily, weekly, or monthly, it is essential to understand that giving value is essential to building a strong relationship.

Here are some tips on cultivating a meaningful, professional relationship with your subscriber:

- **Keep in touch with your mailing list often.** Don't mail them only when you need to promote a product. Let them know when something memorable happens, like you had a baby, or went on a fun trip, or made a funny video. Keep in touch with your subscribers so they will remember you. Not doing so will severely damage any chance of a long-term relationship.

- **Ask about their needs and concerns.** Use surveys and questionnaires to get them involved. Ask them what they want you to provide in order to help them with their problems. If they participate, heed their advice if at all possible, and then send them a free gift or a significant discount on their next purchase.

- **Send them gifts sometimes.** It could be in the form of free reports, blog articles, videos or even free membership access! Make sure you don't trick them into offering something at a discount if you say it is free. Make these freebees valuable and they will look forward to future correspondence.

- **Be personal.** Let them see your human side or your personal life. Make videos of yourself and your team. Include the bloopers.

- **Be educational.** When you impart something of value to your subscribers, they will see you as a teacher and listen to what you say.

If you are not currently building an email list of subscribers, now is the time. Here are the top five email auto-responders that I suggest:

iContact.com
Aweber.com
Infusionsoft.com
Constantcontact.com
Getresponse.com

One last thing when it comes to email marketing:

- **Don't worry about subscribers unsubscribing.** This is just part of engaging people. There will always be people who unsubscribe - don't beat yourself up over it. However, there is a point when too many subscribers are unsubscribing (i.e. over 0.5% opt-out rate) where you might want to analyze your emails and make sure that you are providing relevant content to your subscribers.

WEBINARS

Webinars are becoming more relevant and more mainstream than ever before. With technology improving and internet speeds increasing, it is now easier than ever to produce and deliver powerful webinars.

A webinar is an amazing way to engage your prospects, subscribers and customers. They can hear your voice, see your presentation and feel a part of a community all at one time.

Here are five tips to putting on a great webinar:

Organize – You must plan and organize a productive webinar well in advance of the actual event. Not preparing for the webinar will result in frustrated participants.

Prepare – Get your registrants excited to register and attend the webinar. Be specific with the webinar's content and what the audience will be learning. Make sure you give it a catchy title with the bullet points of what will be learned.

Engage – Plan on engaging your attendees with interesting and valuable information. You must keep the attention of the participants so they don't leave the webinar.

Teach – You need to provide content that informs the audience of ways to improve their lives or businesses. You cannot simply sell; a webinar should be a learning environment.

Follow-up - Schedule your webinar when the greatest number of people can attend. It is very important that you remind the registrants of the upcoming event via email, text message or any other form of communication. The key is to get them to attend. One way to provide exceptional service would be to give them a link of a replay of the webinar that they can use at their discretion.

Here are the top seven current webinar software services I recommend:

Gotowebinar.com
Webex.com
Megameeting.com
Fuzemeeting.com
Adobe Connect 8
Microsoft Office Live Meeting
Skype (for small groups)

You can also offer pre-recorded webinar events. This is where you pre-record your webinar and essentially replay it over and over again. To the registrant, however, it looks like it is live. I suggest Automated Webinar Generator at yourwebinarevent.com/software to run your pre-recorded webinars.

TELESEMINARS

A teleseminar is much like a webinar but it is all audio and no video. It is usually over a phone line where the presenter talks for a certain amount of time on a specific topic. The same rules apply to teleseminars as they do for webinars. The key is to get the registrants to remember that you will be having the call and getting them to join at the correct time. You can also send the replay once you are finished; just remember to record it before you start.

When it comes to teleseminars, the go-to person and hands-down authority is Alex Mandossian. Go to TeleseminarSecrets.com to learn more.

SOCIAL MEDIA

I could write multiple books on the subject of Social Media. In fact, there have been many books already written. The problem with Social Media is that it is constantly changing and will continue to do so as technology and society evolve.

Here are our five rules to social marketing success:

Be consistent
Be authentic
Be conversational
Be informative
Be engaging

Here is the "Don't Be" list:

Don't be all about the numbers
Don't be salesy (I know this isn't a word but you know what I mean)
Don't be fake (people can see right through you)
Don't be impolite
Don't spam
Don't give up

Social media can be one of your most valuable tools to building relationships with your prospects and customers if you do it correctly. The key is to stay consistent and to give massive value. Trying to sell something online can be difficult, but trying to build a valuable relationship is simple. You must give, give, give and then give some more.

One last thing. Don't worry about how many followers, friends, or whatever it's called that you have on any given social channel. You could have millions of followers that could care less about what you are saying. Or you could have 100 followers that devour every word you create. Now that's leverage!

Earlier I mentioned my Building Social Equity 2.0 course. In the course I outline how to use some of the most popular social media platforms out there. Another bonus I share for all members of the online course is the "Vital Elements of a Facebook Fan Page" and some amazing software to help you create an amazing fan page. So yes, it pays to be a member.

DIRECT MAIL

This is something that I am implementing in my business that I believe is going to create the WOW factor. Imagine everyone who buys a product or service from you getting a surprise valuable gift mailed to their home or place of business. For example, suppose I sent all of my followers this book in the mail. Do you think that would build upon an already great relationship, even if they didn't read it? Sure it would.

Even if you simply send a post card in the mail thanking your customer for their purchase you will create the WOW factor. You won't necessarily see the ROI right away, but your relationship with your new customer will begin to improve!

Sendoutcards is a company that I like to use for sending cards and post cards to build relationships. They allow you to pick out a card, write a note and provide an address all online. Then they print the card, put a stamp on it, and mail it for you. You can check them out at Sendoutcards.com/6108.

MAGAZINES

A powerful way to influence and create rapport is by creating a magazine for your followers. The easiest and most affordable way of doing this is by creating an online magazine, sometimes called an e-zine. You must be consistent (I suggest a quarterly magazine) in the creation and distribution, whether you print or email your magazine. You also must send valuable information in each issue or you will be wasting your time and your reader's time.

The way to make the creation process easy is by inviting industry experts or other novelists to write articles for your magazine. This frees up you and/or your staff from having to write all the articles and provides different views and perspectives.

The magazine can eventually become a revenue source by selling advertising. But I suggest you do this sparingly. Remember that the magazine is a tool for creating relationships with your followers and for delivering valuable content.

PODCASTS

Some people don't like to be in front of the video camera. For them, podcasting can be an amazing tool for reaching their audience. Podcasting is online audio content that is delivered by an RSS feed. A good example of this is iTunes, which is essentially an RSS feed of audio shows or content.

Think of podcasting as just another way of reaching your audience. Some people love to listen to their mp3 players while they're exercising, driving, etc. This is a perfect time for them to listen to your podcast.

APPLICATIONS

There are many forms of applications that allow you to engage an audience. Here are just a few examples:

- Mobile applications
- Desktop applications
- Social Media applications
- Browser applications

With an application, you have the ability to send your message quickly and efficiently to grab the attention of your subscribers. There are really no set rules to creating an application, just keep in mind that it becomes a channel that you must consistently manage in order to remain effective.

LIVE STREAMING VIDEOS (Webcasts)

Webcasts are becoming more popular than ever due to services like Ustream.tv and Livestream.com. This can take a bit more technological know-how, but it is becoming easier to use every year. Webcasts allow you to create a TV show that gives you the opportunity to talk about whatever you would like for however long you want. They are extremely powerful!

LIVE EVENTS

In almost every case, there is nothing better than meeting people face to face. This is why live events are one of the most effective ways of building valuable relationships with your market. Live events however can be expensive and usually take a significant amount of time and planning to successfully pull off.

Meetup.com can be a good place to start for creating a live event in your local area. A live event must be well organized and worth someone taking time out of their lives to attend. The rewards are often worth the effort for those that have the ability and charisma to see them through.

There they are: ten ways to build quality relationships while keeping in contact with your followers and readers. I want to emphasize that you do not have to apply all ten of these methods right away to be successful. What I do want you to do is to pick at least two that resonate with your message and then DO THEM CONSISTENTLY!

The truth is that I could write another book just on the subject of marketing a book. Perhaps one day I will. But for now, you have enough tools to start marketing. It doesn't matter which tools or channels you use. What matters is that you are consistent day in and day out.

There are many things you can do after writing your first book. Maybe that includes writing your second book. The amazing thing is that you are now a published author and that places you in a new, revered status that only a few dedicated people hold. I recommend that you don't stop there. Use this to your advantage!

Hopefully I have taken you through a fulfilling journey that has opened your mind to a new awareness of how to write a book ASAP. As a teenager, I never thought in a million years that I would be an author one day. I just didn't believe it was possible. I am now the author of many books with plans to write at least one book a year for the rest of my life.

You see, writing a book is simply a process, much like baking a cake. You put the effort and correct ingredients in and the end result is a beautiful, delicious and rewarding prize.

You can do this! I believe in you! Now show the world that you believe in yourself!

It is your time. Today is the day you choose to finish your book, share it with others and make a difference.

Talk to you soon,

Garrett Pierson

Continuing Education

Although much was discussed in the book "How To Write A Book ASAP," I would like to continue working with you in your quest to finish your book.

As your personal coach, I will take you by the hand and guide you step-by-step through the intimidating and often confusing process of writing your first book.

As a valuable member of my How to Write a Book ASAP Online Training Course, you will receive exclusive and instant access to me, Garrett Pierson, as your mentor. You will also receive a workbook and several volumes of comprehensive, step-by-step video training guides.

Visit **HowToWriteABookASAP.com/Training** today to find out more!

To claim your discount, simply
Scan the QR code above or type this URL
into your browser –
HowToWriteABookASAP.com/Training

**What are you waiting for?
Let's get started today.**

About The Author

Garrett Pierson coaches individuals and businesses in their quest to find what it takes to be successful by motivating them to create the life they deserve and the business they desire. His valuable, insightful tools and techniques make it easy for anyone with personal or business aspirations to reach the previously unattained.

He is founder of **New Generation Consulting, a consulting firm** specializing in search engine optimization, social media, website conversion and online success. Clients include Alex Mandossian, Global Marketing Strategies, Webstarget, ArticlesandSubmissions.com and many more.

Garrett currently runs an online software company with his business partner Scott Brandley. In 2010, Garrett and Scott successfully launched **Shopper Approved**, a fully-automated customer rating and review service that helps website owners create huge amounts of positive social proof which influence, educate, and motivate new customers to buy. They hit another home run in 2011 with the launch of **Rhino Support**, a web-based customer support management system for online businesses.

Garrett is author of the book "**What Success Takes**", a print and audio book on "The Die Hard Principles of True Victory in Life, Business, and Soul." This book includes 30 interviews with successful people such as *Raymond Aaron, Mike Filsaime, Carolyn Ellis, Noah St. John, Joel Comm, Russell Brunson and many more.* He is also the co-author of "**The Trust Factor**" a print and e-book that teaches "7 Strategies To Convert Your Online Visitors Into Lifetime Customers."

Garrett has a passion for helping others. And, one of those passions is in helping others to write their first book and to do it fast. Nothing pleases Garrett more than seeing his students grow socially, psychologically and emotionally by writing and publishing their own books. Garrett is a family centered entrepreneur that lives his passion each and every day. It's his goal to help others do the same.

You can find out more about Garrett Pierson at www.GarrettPierson.com and more about his "How To Write A Book ASAP" training program at www.HowToWriteABookASAP.com/training

NOTES

NOTES

NOTES

Made in the USA
Lexington, KY
21 November 2014